THE EYE OF A LITTLE GOD

G.W. HAWKER

SIX ORDINARY LIVES,
SIX EXTRAORDINARY YEARS.

All rights reserved, no part of this publication may be reproduced or transmitted by any means whatsoever without the prior permission of the publisher.

Edited by Toni Glitz
glitzedit.co.uk

Text © G. W. Hawker

Cover image Ahmad Safarudin
ISBN: 978-1-916756-23-6

Veneficia Publications
July 2024

VENEFICIA PUBLICATIONS UK
veneficiapublications.com

CONTENTS

CHAPTER 1 1

CHAPTER 2 40

CHAPTER 3 78

CHAPTER 4 115

CHAPTER 5 156

CHAPTER 6 194

CHAPTER 7 235

CHAPTER 8 279

CHAPTER 9 324

CHAPTER 1
November 2016

Donald Trump is elected President of the United States, despite losing the popular vote by three million votes.

The Judgement of the High Court is that Brexit must be decided by parliament.

Scientists warn that the world will miss key climate target.

Jon

And so the new term began. Jon Fox was sitting at his desk watching this year's batch of students shuffle into the lecture hall; an annual ritual he had witnessed for fifteen years. As they entered, they quickly scanned around trying to judge which seat to take. It was a game he enjoyed watching: the choice between where was cool to sit and where was safe. Once you had made up your mind, there was no going back. The person you sat with might end up a friend or an enemy or, worse of all, a bore.

Jon was particularly interested in his female students; every year choosing three he would pay particular attention to. There was no hurry. He would see this lot ten times over the course of the academic year. In that time, he would set three essays. There would be tutorials for those who requested them. In some cases, he could recommend a one-to-one if he felt it would be beneficial, educationally or otherwise.

Two minutes to ten and he was on his feet. This, he admitted to himself, was a little power game. He'd never had to bring them to order. He would allow the group, now numbering over fifty, to hush themselves into silence. The longest he'd had to wait was ten minutes. That was the notorious year group the staff had unanimously called the wacky brigade. That year it had been as if all the half-wits and miscreants had somehow bubbled to the surface and presented themselves all at once in one foul genetically-engineered year. This bunch was settling within a few minutes.

"My name is Jon Fox and I'm your entertainment for the year." That always won a laugh. "There was an infinity of time before I was born. There will be an infinity of time after I am gone. How or why my tiny parcel of allotted time means that I stand before you now and in no other time, I cannot say but here I am and there you are, so I suggest we just get on with it."

He started his first lecture with the same observation every year. And every year he could see the effect the words had on his audience. It went over the heads of some students but for the majority, he could see the words amused but also impressed.

Only two students in his fifteen years had spotted that he was paraphrasing Blaise Pascal. One had been a know-it-all called Lawrence Judd. He'd been a pretty boy; pale skin with a turned-up nose and round specs. He may have made it to the top three that year if he hadn't been so brazen and so male. The other had been Esme Holt. She had been the exception in the wacky brigade. As bright a student as ever was. She'd seduced him, not the other way around. Smoking in bed, she had pointed out the plagiarism.

Being caught out had amused him but she hadn't left it at that. She'd started listing other unattributed opinions and explanations he had failed to accredit. He'd ended up putting his hand over her mouth.

"That's enough, methinks." He had attempted to be funny but both had known he was serious. When leaving, she'd stood smiling at the door.

"I'm not upset that you lied; I'm upset that from now on I can't believe you. Friedrich Nietzsche." Despite his countless texts and messages, she never slept with him again.

"Critical Thinking: this module is the key to all other subjects. In this age of misinformation, disinformation and general dawdle in all its guises and forms (flutter of giggles) more than anything, second only to the air you breathe, you need critical thinking. What do we mean by the term critical thinking?" A girl in the second row stuck her hand in the air. "Please put your hand down. This isn't school. I was actually asking a rhetorical question but let's hear your answer anyway."

"It's about making sound sense of the information you have in front of you."

"Not right but not bad. What's your name please?"

"Immy Marshall."

With her long, untied hair and her oversized glasses, she went straight into the top three, pending revision.

"Immy," he said, not entirely removing the smirk from his voice. "You have some of the essence. Critical thinking is the ability to analyse information objectively and thereupon make a reasoned judgement. If you make it to the end of the course and don't do the sensible thing and jack it all in to go and train as a barista or a retail assistant, you will hopefully mature into critical thinkers. You will be able to appraise the calibre of the information which comes your way. You will thus solve problems effectively and make reasonable and balanced decisions. The opposite has been demonstrated recently by the voting habits of our American cousins, who now have—and I think deserve—a game-show host as president *(the best laugh so far)*. Before we go on, you may have heard that I ban pens, notebooks and electronic scribbling pads from my lectures. I want you to listen, absorb and think."

"Surely, we can do that and make notes."

Ah, the smartass has emerged! Only a matter of time. It was a lanky bastard in the back row, his hair deliberately scruffy.

"Let's give my idea a try first, shall we?"

"Could we record you then?"

"So I'd end up on YouTube being dubbed to a Little Mix song? I don't think so."

More laughter—a knowing smile from Immy. He continued with his introduction until, about forty minutes in, his phone lit up with a message from his wife. Lynda wrote texts in the style of telegrams: *Bonkers is dead—involved in collision with double deck bus—can you pick up another one before Sophie realises?*

"I can see some of you are losing the will to live. Get used to that feeling. Assimilating knowledge is an exhausting business. If you have any doubts, look at Bilbo Baggins. You all have access to the book list online. Maybe take a peep before our next meeting."

He had rather liked Bonkers, the ginger cat they had taken in three years ago. Typical solution of Lynda's: dismiss, replace, move on. He recently noted that his older daughter, Victoria, was taking on some of his wife's deplorable traits, but Sophie, his youngest, was the opposite. Surely, they'd need to give him a decent burial rather than immediately substitute him with another. Sophie would be cool with that. She was seven and needed to learn about life and death, after all.

On the way out, he asked Kay, the receptionist, where he could get a ginger cat from.

"A cat shop—where else?"

"Thank you, Miss Honeybun. Very helpful."

Lexi

The mysterious illness arrived on November 2nd, 2016. It came without warning or fanfare.

The day before, everything had been perfectly normal. Maybe Lexi Morgan's mum had come home a few minutes earlier than usual. Maybe her dad had arrived home a tad later. Her sister Sara had been playing her music at max volume, thudding through her closed door. Moreover, the dog, had been sick twice on the stairs. Her brother, Harry, had slipped on the pool of vomit and had retaliated by kicking him hard. This had precipitated a shouting match between Lexi and Harry. Perfectly normal.

With everyone friends by dinnertime, her dad had been saving a joke to share as soon as they had been sitting down.

"Why can't you trust atoms?" His jokes had always been terrible and cringe-worthy but if he hadn't had one, they'd been disappointed. "Because they make up everything!" They had giggled and snorted but their dad had always laughed the most. That particular day though Harry had come back with a counter-gag.

"What did one wall say to another?"

Both father and son sang out the answer. "I'll meet you in the corner!" Sara had required an explanation, which had rather taken the shine off it.

Lexi had left the family watching television to go to her room. TV had been boring and there had seemed to be only one programme on at the moment; a programme called Brexit. Anyway, she'd had science homework. She'd had no intention of doing it and had set her morning alarm for twenty minutes earlier. In the morning she would jump straight out of bed, puke out enough rubbish about motion theory to know when a one-ton car travelling at fifty kilometres an hour should brake to avoid hitting an old woman crossing the road.

No, her objective had been to get on Facebook and track down a new boy in her class, Jayden Swift. All the other boys were losers compared to this lad. He seemed older than his years, quiet but confident, a wave of black hair falling over his dark eyes. An hour later, she had found nothing. In desperation, she had phoned her mate Freya. After getting Freya to swear on the lives of her entire family including pets, she had asked her to help in the search for Jayden. Another hour had ticked by before Freya had phoned back.

"Nada, zilch, fuck all. Checked Instagram as well as Twitter. It appears Jayden Swift only exists in that weird place called reality."

It may possibly have been Halloween that explained the arrival of the illness. Her grandmother had once said that should you misbehave, the dead are always happy to step in with a curse. But Halloween had been and gone. Even if it hadn't gone, while she did believe in her grandmother's tendency to make mischief, the notion that the dead could curse was nonsense.

She would have weeks and months and years to think about the possible reason for the sudden illness. Nothing ever made sense. At three she'd woken up after falling asleep with a smile on her face. Jayden's existence / non-existence had only served to deepen her fascination with him. Lexi had reached over for her glass of water, taken a sip, and gone directly back to her favourite dream: by stroking the air, she had the ability to float at will.

The mysterious illness arrived at around six in the morning. It didn't knock. It found the front door unlocked. It drifted up the stairs and bypassed all the other bedrooms until it arrived at Lexi's door.

Without hesitation, it opened it, lifted the covers and got into bed with the sleeping child.

The alarm went off at six-fifty. Lexi immediately noticed something was wrong. The left side of her body was not so much stiff and unmoving, as absent. She couldn't feel a thing. Commanding her left arm to rise up met with no response. Her toes wouldn't wriggle. The right side was how it had been the previous night; everything worked as expected. She didn't panic or cry out but she lay there trying to breathe normally. She spied her homework open at the correct page on her desk with nobody to solve the problem of how to stop the car hitting the poor old woman crossing the road.

She attempted to pull herself together, to stop being fucking silly and get her arse out of bed. She ended up on the floor. Her upper body, obviously the most determined part, ended up on the carpet, her legs still in bed. This is how they found her. Sara opened the door first, looking for socks and stopped short on seeing her sister.

"What you doing?"

Lexi was tempted to say she was looking for her phone which had slipped under the bed. "I think you'd better get Mum."

Minutes later the whole family was in her room, her dad rushing forward to put her back in bed.

"What you playing at, Lexi?" was her mum's worried response. "Get ready for school and stop messing about."

"It's my left side. I can't move it."

Her mum tried one more if-you're-buggering-us-about comment but was silenced by the look on her husband's face.

"I think we need to phone the doctor, Kate."

Her mum rounded up the other two and told her dad to take them to school. She would phone in sick while she waited for the doctor. Once the audience had gone, her mum went over her body, systematically tapping every square inch of flesh.

"Can you feel that? Can you feel this?" The numbness, her mother found, was indeed confined to her left hand, arm, hip, leg and foot. Her right side was fine, normal; her face was fine, normal.

The doctor ran his own fingers up and down her and agreed with her mum's findings.

"Yes, paralysis of the left side."

"And?" her mother asked, after a pause which was far too long, given the circumstance.

"Could be many explanations."

"And?"

"Some sort of palsy. I'm quite sure this is temporary and everything will soon be back to working order. However, as a precaution, I think we need to get Lexi checked out in hospital."

It was while waiting for the ambulance that Lexi started to react emotionally to what was happening. Up until then, she had been calm, almost passive, as if she were in a movie. Tears began to flow down her cheeks. Her mum responded likewise and used the same tissue to dry both of their tears.

Her mum's words, 'it'll be alright', triggered the first scream from Lexi. By the time the ambulance arrived, she had been screaming for ten minutes. Her mother, afraid of being near her, was happy to allow them to wrap her up, belt her into the stretcher and take her away. She would follow later with some things—an act her husband, David, would later admonish her for.

Truth be told, she needed a minute. As soon as the front door banged shut, she fell on her knees and prayed to a god she'd never prayed to and didn't believe in. She called him Jesus in a bid to make it personal.

Dexter

You never know what will happen in a day. Dexter Jennings opened the shop up at ten, sharp. This meant turning the sign from *Shut Happens* to *Come In—We're Awesome!*

He went back to his black coffee, three shots, and picked up the newspaper he had been reading. He questioned why he was bothering: the news was 99% Brexit. Surely it should be only 52% reflecting the result. It had been five months since the vote and they still hadn't sorted anything out yet. He pushed the paper to one side and glanced over to his diary: 2pm a stylized star on the arm, 3.30pm a snake collar. Routine stuff. He had been in the trade for years and publicised himself as the best tattooist on the south coast.

Frankie Claxton opened the door and stood there holding the door wide, "I want a tattoo."

"Shame," he rejoined automatically, "I only do nails."

"Very funny. Where do you want me?"

"Normally," Dexter said, guzzling back his coffee, "I offer a pre-appointment for anything which takes more than an hour."

"Let's have our pre-appointment appointment then."

Dexter realised that he wasn't going to get away with this one. Grabbing the diary once again it confirmed what he already knew.

"Okay, what do you want, where do you want it and when?"

"A butterfly. On my tits. Now," she said, lighting up a cigarette. Frankie ignored his request to stub out the fag. "Is that the pre-appointment appointment over?"

Dexter struggled to come up with any further questions.

"Have you any idea what sort of butterfly?"

"Do you think I would come to you unprepared? Here, look at that beauty." She retrieved a screwed-up picture from her hip pocket.

"Adonis Blue."

"Spot on. You do know your stuff after all. I would like the blue to be darker and the edge to be red, not white."

"So really not the Adonis blue?"

"But exactly the one I have carried in my head all year."

"And you say you want it on your breasts?"

"Yes, my tits." Before she could lift up her T-shirt, he suggested they went into the back room.

He turned the sign back to *Shut Happens*.

"Bloody hell, it reeks in here."

"Antiseptics. We keep a clean shop here. Before we go any further, I would like to point out our tattooist code on respect and privacy."

"Look, can you do my Adonis or not?"

"I think I can."

"You can, or you think you can?"

"I can."

With that she whipped off her T-shirt and traced her finger around her breasts, "One blue wing for each."

"I have to ask the question. Do you realise that once done, always done?"

She looked mystified. "What other reason would I want it done?"

By ten thirty, his beloved Ghost Shader Hybrid was in operation and Frankie Claxton, whose real name he found out was Tara Smith, was loving every minute of it. No pain, no gain.

This was the sort of challenge he loved. A bold and beautiful image on the pale and delicate flesh of a woman's body. He liked to work in silence, his motto being 'Ink is meditation'. For a half hour or so, Frankie was happy to chain-smoke her way through her discomfort.

When he was colouring around one of her nipples, she started a conversation.

"How did you vote?"

"Remain. Why rock the boat?"

"You're a fool."

"Just to remind you, I'm the one with the needle here."

"Let me give you a quick history lesson. We won the war, yes or no?" She didn't wait for an answer. "And yet, which country is the most powerful in Europe? Germany. When they realised it was all going belly up in 1945, they formulated an alternative plan. With the Jews."

"Well, that's ridiculous."

"Not so. Their thing they had about the Jews was always about money and power. After the war they needed money to hatch their new plan. To dominate Europe."

"That's ridiculous."

"You keep saying that but look at the evidence. Do your own research and see what you come up with. As part of their vision and not a part of ours, we have become a serf state to the Fuhrer."

"Ridiculous."

"Don't you see that's what they want you to believe? A vote to remain was a vote for the status quo and a vote for the status quo would have been a vote for domination."

Her breasts were magnificent and to Dexter they had been made specifically to be adorned by the Adonis Blue or, to be more precise, the version that had been created in Frankie Claxton's mind. He used ocean blue, rich and depthless, contrasted with crimson edging. For the butterfly's body he took a risk and coloured it with Tuscan sun.

As she talked away, filling in the details of why he should have voted leave and not remain, he could see his work of art emerging on her body like a silent song. Three hours later he sat back sharing a cigarette with Frankie. She was sitting back, completely unashamed, her breasts still uncovered but now glowing with Dermalize Protective Film. Although the butterfly remained captured and subdued, he could see that this was his Michelangelo moment.

"May I take a photograph?"

"Help yourself."

He stopped at thirty pictures, although Frankie was up for thirty more. "You have amazing tits, you know."

"Does the Tattooist code say you can say that?" she challenged, playing with him.

"Is it painful? How does it feel?"

"Like I have been thrown from a motorcycle at a hundred miles an hour and skidded on my boobs."

"Ouch! Plus, I'm charging you two hundred quid for the experience."

"Worth every penny, Mr Tattoo man."

My god, it had taken all morning. The stylised star was due in twenty minutes. Rather formally, they shook hands as she left.

"Don't forget what I said. We're totally much better off outside Europe. By the way, have you any kids?"

"Yes, two."

"Well, at least they will have a better chance now we're out. And don't get the poor fuckers vaccinated, for Christ's sake."

If he wasn't so overwhelmed by his morning's work, his head reeling with the diatribe of her beliefs, he would say he was mildly concussed. He went into the small courtyard outside his workshop. He just had to smoke a joint and, as he did so, he looked through the photographs on his phone. Twice. Great tits.

Alright, one stylised star coming up, the star of David, the star of Bethlehem, the star of stars.

He splashed water on his face, walked through his shop, his studio, his study of dreams and turned the sign; *Come In—We're Awesome!*

Ursula

Sometimes Ursula Bird wondered who was actually in charge: her or these bloody pets she had accumulated over the years? Every single movement, even thinking about making a move, and the three dogs would stir. Ahmed, the Jack Russell, would be first on the case, whacking his tail enthusiastically. Carlo, the half-poodle/half-something else, would try to usurp Ahmed's position by annoyingly jumping up and down.

It broke her heart to watch Desmond, an ancient Labrador, struggle to his feet, a mechanical replica of his former self but determined not to be outdone by the youngsters. More often than not, he would finally get to his feet to discover that Ursula had only moved from one cheek of her ass to the other.

It didn't stop there. Mousey, the mouse, took to her wheel and two of her three cats shot up. Harriet was first up, meowing for food regardless of the time of day. Basil lurked around in the background, wary of the dogs although they never showed him any attention. Leo was the only animal here with any sense. This domestic drama was way beneath him. He would be somewhere outside in the real world, up a tree or in a skip or down the allotment, daubing insects with his indifferent paw. That day she may see him, she may not.

But today was Thursday. Tomorrow was bin day so there was something that needed to be done. She placed her neat gin on the table—she had forgotten to buy the tonic—and placed the marker in her book, *A Little Life* which in her opinion should be renamed *A Long Read*.

"A maiore ad minus," Ursula announced to her groupies. "For your benefit, Carlo: from the greater to the smaller."

Ursula duly led the caravan of dogs and cats out to the curb. Every time, without exception and much to her own annoyance, she would say the same old thing.

"In my day, there was only one bin, now there's a triplet of bins: food waste, recyclables and actual rubbish. There must be easier ways to save the planet."

As soon as she opened the door, the dogs pushed through enthusiastically in order to empty their bladders. The air was crisp and cool against her bare arms. The pink moon was half hidden behind a cloud. A dancer in a skirt, she mused. She touched the tree in her garden as part of this weekly ritual.

Once she had written that trees are giants who show their wisdom by choosing not to speak. The tree's life did have the air of secrecy about it: a tree is never elsewhere; it is always here and now.

She looked up and down the road. Not a soul about. A fox furtively crossed the road further down. She looked down at her dogs. Not one of her daft mutts reacted. The cats pretended to see nothing. The fox stopped, sniffed the air, and deciding her little band was not a threat, walked off at the same pace.

Back in the house, she decided it was time for bed. She downed the remainder of the gin, placed a tea towel over Mousey's cage, collected her glass of milk from the kitchen and climbed the stairs. Like a well-practised routine, now five years in the making, the contingency of pets followed her up to the bedroom, ready to take up their positions for the night.

In the bedroom, she lit the candle for him on a special table in the corner. This was her only reminder of him. She kept the candle going, not so much as a show of respect or an act of commemoration but as a reminder of what was important.

Long ago she had decided to put all her photographs of him on the disused barbeque.

"Any words?" she had asked the dogs. "No, nor have I."

She'd lit the first one, their wedding day, and she'd watched the flames flow through the years: holidays, anniversaries, garden parties, dinners with friends. All joined in the celebrations, their faces contorting, colours swelling, corners browning and the inevitable lapse into ash. She'd never told anyone she had done this. They may have found it strange rather than seeing it for what it really represented: an atonement.

While Desmond was still taking the stairs, a gentle thud as every step was breached, Carlo and Ahmed had already found their places on the bed. Harriet was on the pillow formerly reserved for the man of the house and Basil was probably in the wardrobe.

This was her favourite time of the day. Ursula got her notebook out and continued writing the short story she was currently working on. She had rejected computers as a way of capturing her words—too clinical—and further back still, she had smashed her old Erika typewriter in a fit of youthful angst. She'd told friends at the time that it was like trying to write in a field of galloping horses. She'd gone back to good old writing by hand. Her grammar-school handwriting was elegant and seductive and gave her words the gravitas they deserved.

To date, she had published five novels, two books of short stories and a partly illustrated volume of her collected poems 1978–2011. Despite years of trying, years of accruing a bookshelf of plastic wallet files crammed with rejection slips, every one of her works was self-published. Ursula couldn't really explain why. In 1980, Charles Causley, the Cornish poet, had said that her poetry was gutsy and vivid. On a course a few years later, Kazuo Ishiguro had told her that her narratives were original and engaging and that all she had to do was carry on writing.

Well, she had carried on writing. Those who had read her work enjoyed it, or had said they did, but the readership had rarely gone beyond a few hundred. Needless to say, Robert had hated her writing. He couldn't understand why she was wasting her time. "Nobody reads them anyway."

She'd taken no notice. He had been an intellectual cretin and in brave moments she'd told him as much to his face. The Sun newspaper was the only literature he'd known and, she'd added, that was written for people with a reading age of eight. She hadn't been sure about that but it made no difference anyway.

    She woke up to Ahmed licking her face. She had overslept, the sun already peeping through her curtains. Ahmed was probably dying to pee. She could hear the bins being emptied. She looked over her notes from the night before. Maybe, a thousand words. She wasn't a hundred percent sure where she was going with it but she could feel that the new story was finally taking shape.

Matthew

Matthew Price had bought a jiffy bag especially. As was his way, he decided to make a bit of an occasion of it. He had been saving the bottle of 2014 Sun & Moon Pinot Noir for a future celebration and decided this was it.

He read a couple of his favourite poems and was almost at the point of saying a small prayer when he had to stop himself. He laughed. God's little joke. He took a sip of the wine and he was back in New Zealand. After walking all day with Joy, they had descended into Queenstown, stopping at the first bar. She had ordered the wine, he a lager, but when she'd insisted, he'd tasted it; it had been the oral equivalent of an orgasm. He hadn't shared that particular metaphor with Joy, but he'd set the lager aside and ordered a bottle. He had been ordering bottles ever since.

On his second glass he formally took off his clerical collar, which he had been comically wearing with his pyjamas. He couldn't be bothered to get dressed and, as this little ritual was literally for his eyes only, he knew it didn't matter. On the collar he wrote: *I'm singing to the silence instead*. He didn't sign it. The Bishop would guess who it was from. He had intended to place his certificates of qualification and ordination with it but they were in a suitcase somewhere in his attic and he had nobody to get them down for him. He kissed the collar and sealed it into the envelope.

Ah, a sudden surprise of tears. Didn't expect that! Time for another glass.

Matthew's first and only spiritual experience had come when he was twelve years old. He'd been laid out in bed trying to catch his breath. He had been diagnosed with asthma as a baby. His mother had loved telling the story, to whoever would listen, of how he would have died but for a nurse who, for six long hours, manually used a plastic pump to get oxygen into his tiny lungs. It had been the last month of the war and his mother had welled up when telling her tale, believing that her first born was symbolic of a new life to come.

His childhood had been a litany of sick notes: Matthew couldn't jump, run, play football, or climb ropes. School years had been peppered with weeks in bed, sipping soup, drinking Lucozade, his chest clammy with Vicks VapoRub. Occasionally, if the inhaler failed, Dr Mansfield would be called. After the usual breath in/breath out exploration with the stethoscope, he would slip a yellow tablet under Matthew's tongue. The effect had been almost instant and always ecstatic. It had been like being out at sea, being tossed about relentlessly, one wave after another and then being hoisted onto land, everything becoming calm and solid. His breathing had eased and like falling into honey, he had sunk into a dreamless sleep.

And there he had been, aged twelve, in bed again panting for breath. His mother had visited him on the hour, refreshed his drink, puffed up his pillow, placed a new cold flannel on his forehead and then hovered around biting her lip.

"If you're no better by tomorrow, it's Dr Mansfield for you, Matthew Price."

As the night had begun to ooze into his bedroom, his body rigid and his fists clenched, he had felt someone loosen his grip and take his hand. His shock had been mitigated by the fact that his breathing had immediately relaxed and a cool sensation had flowed through his body, his face softening, his mind emptying.

"Who are you?"

"Close your eyes. Sleep."

And that had been it. Not exactly choirs of angels, or God on his throne, or the burning bush, or a light at the end of a tunnel. Yet, in the morning, he'd woken up without any symptoms. His mother hadn't believed it. When she'd crept in at eight, Matthew had been on the bed, already dressed for school, knotting his tie.

"It's a miracle!" she'd exclaimed. All day those words had stayed with him. It had been a miracle; it had been miraculous. At that point, he hadn't grabbed a bible but a dictionary. A miracle: an extraordinary and welcome event not explicable by natural or scientific laws and therefore attributed to a divine agency. He'd been a walking miracle and had grinned his way through the first day back at school.

Sixty-five years later and the dog collar he'd longed to have as soon as he'd left school—the dog collar which denoted endless hours of prayer and study, debate and ceremony—was now in a jiffy bag ready for posting.

"Easy come, easy go," he joked aloud. "What now? Ah, yes, another glass of red, if you don't mind."

He was raising the third glass to his lips, when someone inconveniently knocked on the door. He shouted for them to come in.

"Only me!" It was Fiona. She appeared at the doorway to the lounge.

"I must be losing my marbles. I didn't realise it was your day."

"No, your marbles are still intact. I'm on the way to the shops and wondered if you need anything. More wine, maybe?"

"Well-spotted, Fiona. Want a glass?"

"Driving, I'm afraid. So, you don't want nought? I don't want you to run out of anything. For reasons which are beyond me, people have started panic buying, apparently stockpiling in case it's a hard Brexit, whatever that may mean."

"You could post this for me," he said, handing her the envelope.

"Looks very official. Oh, the Bishop of Salisbury. Not another begging letter?"

Fiona was excellent at making him laugh. She had been helping him for three years now, three days a week. It was an arrangement that worked well. He did what he could but she could do everything faster and more thoroughly. Apart from that, she was such a live wire and never failed to cheer him up.

Later, while heating his meal, he reflected as to whether his gesture to the bishop was too theatrical and unnecessary. Yes, he concluded, it was both theatrical and unnecessary but it was the act of a free man, uncollared and unchained. All those pointless scrapes with God throughout his life until he'd finally realised he had been shadow-boxing all the time. The murder had been the final straw.

Tia

Today was Friday. Benefits were due on Monday. That translated to eight meals for Tia Hearn and her two children: twenty-four individual servings. She opened her purse. Ten pounds and sixty-four pence. With no other treats, that was forty-four pence per meal. She actually enjoyed doing the maths. Not forgetting of course that they already had some supplies—cereal, rice, two cans of beans—this was more than adequate.

"Plenty," she announced to Galway, their solitary goldfish who, as if in agreement, changed direction to swim clockwise. "I agree more than plenty."

To celebrate she rolled the thinnest roll-up, so thin she knew it would last her only a minute or so if she was lucky. This was her favourite time of the week. Nara was at school and unbeknown to her dad, Kojo spent Fridays with her mum. Tia helped out at a local coffee shop on Friday mornings for a couple of hours, cash-in-hand. £40 every month. In theory she should have declared it but asking no questions, the owner had been happy enough with this arrangement. From the time she arrived home until she had to go and pick Nara up, she had approximately three hours to herself.

Tia was studying. She was fascinated by the human mind. She liked to think about the human brain: that you could hold it in your hand and yet it contained 86 billion neurons and within them they held every memory, thought and feeling you ever had. Her friends had learnt to tolerate what they affectionately called a Tia-ism. If she went on too much, they simply told her to shut up and down her Prosecco.

Her studying was a slightly random, disorganised affair, mostly determined by what she could pick up in a charity shop. She had bought a jumbo notebook and jotted things down if she came across an interesting point or something of worth popped into her mind. She had read Psychology for Dummies — it had cost her 50 pence — and concluded that there were so many theories about the mind that nobody could be certain what was going on. But this excited rather than disappointed her. She'd read Victor Frankl's book *Man's Search for Meaning* and agreed with the basic concept that perception is everything.

She was now reading Carl Jung's *Memories, Dreams and Reflections*. She was only on the *School Years* chapter but what intrigued her was the wealth of thought and imagination he'd been struggling with at such an early age. Her life had been undeniably ordinary compared with his. She had never wrestled with God, questioned her parents or struggled with her existence.

Tia had fallen pregnant with Nara weeks before her sixteenth birthday. Everyone had assumed the father was her old boyfriend, Steve McGarvey but she knew she wasn't his. The baby's father was Mr Fairfax, the Art Teacher. He had begged her not to say anything; he was happily married with four children, he had his career. Apparently, the whole affair was a terrible accident. An accident, she thought to herself, which had happened at least a dozen times in his car, in various school cupboards and once actually in the classroom minutes before the bell rang. In the end, much to her dad's fury, she'd refused to tell anyone who the father was. She still hadn't.

And then her dad had almost blown a gasket when he'd visited the hospital to discover her second child, Kojo, was black. And Tia was barely twenty.

"What the fuck are you doing? Trying to start a chess set? At least choose a fucking English name like Peter or Mark or Joseph."

"They're all Jewish names, Dad."

"All I can say is that you are setting a fine example for Kira. She should be able to look up to her older sister."

It was obvious which way he had voted in the referendum. Nigel Hearn was suspicious of anyone who had been born north of the Bristol Channel or South of the English Channel. Any differences in language, faith or colour terrified the man and he consequently believed anything that confirmed his view of the world.

Watching her husband gear himself up for one of his famous rants, her mum had ushered him away. Even as he'd been leaving the ward he'd had still managed a cheap pop at his daughter's sexual habits. When her mum had returned though, she was all smiles. "He is a real beauty," she'd said.

Kojo's dad had been Ghanaian, although he was known as Micky. He had insisted on Kojo's name before disappearing into the ether. Micky's phone had gone dead; his flat had been emptied and a mutual friend had been apparently clueless as to his whereabouts. She'd assumed—and half-hoped—the Home Office had scooped him up and flown him back to Kumasi.

A knock on the door; it was Pete from upstairs. She was very good at ignoring the obvious fact that he fancied her. He was handsome enough and about her age but he was a druggie and was forever on the lookout for something, anything that promised a moment of oblivion.

"Hi, Tia!" She could tell by the way he sang out her name that he was after money. "I don't suppose I could borrow a couple of quid?" It was pointless asking why he needed the cash. It would be one of what Pete called the holy trinity of alcohol, fags or drugs. "Will pay you back first thing next week." He had never paid her back. "Just two little pounds and I'll be made up."

She dropped the coins into his hand. "That's the lot, Pete. See you Monday," she said, knowing there was more chance of seeing the Buddha on Monday.

On closing the door, she could hear Pete already knocking on the door of the old man living next to her. Unlike her father, Pete made no discrimination when trying to get money: he would have been happy asking the devil for change.

Tia packed away her notes and book and placed them in a kitchen drawer the children were forbidden from going into. She enjoyed the walk to Nara's school. Often, she would meet up with some of the other mums as they made their way to pick up their offspring. If she didn't, the walk was pleasant, through a park, up a hill and into the school. As she reached the gates, something she had read an hour before suddenly arrived in her head and made complete sense. Before she forgot, she typed in the thought into her phone.

"Texting, are we?"

It was Penny, James's mum. Another lone parent, who was obsessed with finding a partner. At any one time, she was on half a dozen dating sites. So far, she had met Mr Right three times, shagged a few married men and had been treated for crabs. Tia had to admit, she had staying power and never failed to remain positive. As a kind of validation, she wanted Tia to join in the search but Tia made excuses, usually around the children. Bottom-line, she wasn't interested in dating—trying to make sense of the young Carl Jung's number one and number two personality attracted her attention like no man could.

Nara was running towards her, arms open and a smile to die for. Tia spun her around a couple of times.

"How was school?"

"Okay."

Halfway home, Nara would suddenly open up and relive the day's mundane events in amazing detail, only stopping when they reached the house.

"That sounds better than okay."

"I'll give it a six out of ten," Nara said after some thought. "Six and a half, max."

CHAPTER 2
April 2017

Theresa May calls a general election to secure a better Brexit deal with an anticipated increased majority.

100 days into Trump's presidency, the wall between Mexico and the US has yet to be started.

Driest 10 months in England for 100 years.

Jon

By the time Jon Fox was on the twelfth essay, he was already going insane. The standard was dismally poor and nowhere near the level he would have expected at this stage. Agreed, it wasn't the most exciting of subjects—Critique the contribution of Paulo Freire to Critical Pedagogy—but it was the necessary portal to what came next.

So far everyone had described Freire's work rather than critiquing it—the whole point of the course, by the way. Not one had omitted the obvious quote in which Freire contrasts the traditional model of likening the student to an empty vessel with his own idea that learning should instead treat the student as a co-creator of knowledge.

Jon looked at the pile to his left: Jesus, thirty-two to go; thirty-two variations on a monotonous theme.

A swell of boredom and before he could censure himself, he googled *Erotic Beauty*. His failing willpower was instantly revived by a Jacob's ladder of angels, ascending and descending his screen. He was becoming fidgety when his telephone, and consequently him, jumped into life. It was Helen, Head of Department. As was her obsession, she was checking to see if any of his students were heading for a re-sit or, heaven forbid, a fail.

Looking at the uneven piles, he wanted to taunt her and say something radical, such as setting fire to the whole lot would offend even Vulcan. This was pure politics. The more he passed the better the course appeared, the better the university looked. If he failed too many, it would put potential students off, which would have an adverse effect on the university's budget. On the other hand, it was an unspoken rule that you had to fail one or two to show it wasn't too much of an easy touch.

Just to wind her up, he told her that at this point, there may be nine or ten who may struggle. A short pause—he imagined her screwing up her lips as was her habit when she became anxious.

"That many? Do you think we need to implement that TIE Input protocol?"

Still scrolling through the naked seraphim, he was about to ask what the fuck the TIE Input protocol was, when he remembered. It was the bollocks they had inexplicably agreed at the end of the last staff meeting: Timely Interim Enhanced Input. In language favoured by the common man: give them some extra help before they fuck up completely!

"Excellent idea, Helen." he said, clicking on the cover picture of Mara, who was laying on her side with nothing but a snake tattoo slithering up her left side. "I'm on the case as we speak."

"Brilliant. I'm determined our results will be the best ever this year."

"More chance of Donald Trump becoming president of the United States." As usual, his sad attempt to introduce humour into the conversation fell on the fallow ground that was Helen Elliot.

He had no sooner finished the call, when there was a knock on the door. He clicked the page off. To his surprise and relief, in walked Immy Marshall.

"Immy," he said, pointing to the seat on the other side of his desk. "How can I help you?"

"I see you're marking our essays. I'm not at all happy with mine and wondered if I may withdraw it?"

"A little extreme, don't you think? I haven't reached yours yet." He shuffled through the pile until he found her assignment. "So, you want it back?"

"I do, I really do," she said, using her index finger to slide her glasses up her nose.

"I have a better idea."

Much to her muted horror, he started to read it there and then. She tried to stop him a couple of times but he showed her the palm of his hand and continued reading. Although Immy thought she would pass out, it only took five minutes. On finishing it, he slapped it down between them.

"Sorry Immy, I'm not allowing you to take it back."

Her face looked like she had just seen a puppy drown. Anticipating tears, he moved on quickly.

"This is fucking brilliant. For a start, you answered the question, something sadly missed by others. But not only that, you provided some truly original thinking about his work. This could well be published. Well done you!" Anticipating tears of a different kind, Jon continued quickly. "Look, what are you doing now? I have a couple of books back at my place. We could have a coffee there and talk about your next step."

Sitting in the car with Immy in the passenger seat, Jon was trying to contain his excitement. He was talking too much and possibly too forcedly, but the objective here was to maintain her interest and stop her from thinking too much. Every now and then he touched her on the arm, ostensibly to emphasise a point but actually to test boundaries.

His first 'conquest' that year had been an abject failure. Grace Carver had been quiet, chubby, and although academically bright, had been inexperienced and timid. Totally unresistant, the sex had been a case of going through the motions. When the thought that she may be a virgin had come into his mind, he'd been quick to dismiss the idea with a few self-made explanations of his own. There would be no second time. Receiving no response from Jon, to his great relief, Grace texted him that she had rekindled her relationship with her former boyfriend.

They drew up outside the house. Before he could turn the engine off, Stanley, Bonkers' replacement, jumped onto the bonnet of the car. Much to their relief, his meowing for attention made both of them laugh.

As they were giggling, Jon noticed that parked alongside his wife's Toyota, there was a strange car on his drive. A Mercedes Benz E-class in red. The only person he knew who drove one of those was that bore at the club. What was his name? David Pratt. Pratt the Twat. He leaned forward and looked up at the bedroom window. The blinds were shut.

"Change of plan," he said. "There's a neat little cafe down the road. It's a cool place which has come out as pro-remain. They got a brick through their window last week. We can have our chat there."

"How about the books?"

"I'll bring them in tomorrow."

They drove in silence; for any number of reasons, a look of disappointment on both of their faces.

Lexi

It was exactly five months since Lexi had fallen out of bed and screamed all the way to the hospital. Since that time, she had learnt to keep it to herself. When she'd alerted her mum on the three-month anniversary, her mum had snapped.

"Shall I bake a cake to celebrate?"

She had apologised later, but Lexi had understood that she had to watch what she said to her. Nobody wanted to be reminded of heartbreak.

Her condition had changed since that first incident. The paralysis had seemed to move to the rest of her body but in doing so, its intensity had been diluted and it had become more of a generalised frailty. She could manage some movement but every muscle protested and a wave of inertia fell on her like a lead weight.

On Lexi's return from the seven interminable days in hospital, her bedroom had felt like she'd left one prison for another. It had felt like the room of some strange child who, filling the shelves up with dolls and figurines, must have been hopelessly immature and puerile. Those books had seemed ridiculously childish, as had the rag doll on top of the chest of drawers. And who, in their right mind, would have asked their father to paint the walls crimson red? She hadn't been able to bear looking at all that junk and had longed for the sinking sun with its promise of oblivion.

Despite the most unusual event of her life so far, the family had somehow accommodated their shock and established a new routine. This routine meant that everyone did what they had done before but now with an almost religious homage, whereby each would enter her room at specific times. And, whereas previously the family had mostly forgotten each other until they were right there in front of them, they had now created a capacity, a sort of hushed space in their head where Lexi resided. Every second of every minute they were aware that Lexi was upstairs in bed, waiting for the little tap on the door, followed by the turn of the handle, a concerned face appearing in the crack.

Her mum would always appear first. Cup of tea in hand, she would scoot across the room, putting on her busy face, trying to be normal. She would invariably pull back the curtains and open the window. She would ask how she had slept and Lexi would respond with a good or an okay. For a reason Lexi had never understood, her mum would fuss about the bed, pulling the sheet tight, puffing up quilts and pillows.

Second up would be her dad. He too would be unnecessarily upbeat and armed with a joke. Lexi would dutifully laugh or roll her eyes if it was too bad. Harry would literally pop his head right through the doorway, ask her how she was, give her a thumbs-up and disappear. Sara would be last. She must have asked her mum what she should do or say, because Sara either had a prepared question about her homework—often made-up, Lexi surmised—or had wanted to borrow or lend her something trivial.

The last item on the daily schedule was when Moreover, the dog, having been walked, fed and watered, had been allowed in her room. Moreover seemed to be the only one capable of a real authentic connection. The Border Terrier greeted her every day as if he hadn't seen her for months. He'd jump onto the bed and lick her until Lexi had had enough. She would catch his little earnest face between her hands as best she could and tell him to calm down. Moreover would settle himself into a comfortable position against her and lie there until later when he'd hear the key turn in the front door latch, then he'd gruff out a sniffled bark and dart out of the room to greet Lexi's mum arriving home.

Since being rushed to hospital, she had been prodded and poked by an army of professionals. Every one of them had posited their theory but not one had come up with anything resembling a solution. Having been through the obstacle course of specialist intervention, Lexi could clearly see there had been an unspoken order. First up had been the search for a physical explanation: weight, heart rate, hormones, enzymes, blood pressure. Next had come the exploration of possible neurological causes: epilepsy, seizures, muscle coordination, dizziness, confusion. When nothing had been found there, they had wondered if it was psychological. Had she been traumatised or abused? Was there evidence of unresolved grief or free-floating anxiety? Was she school phobic or being bullied? Disappointingly for those involved, including her family, every box had remained unticked.

The final grasp at an explanation had been psychiatry. Strangely, any other explanation would have been preferred. The psychiatrist had been a small, charming man from Mauritius. Over three visits, he had spent hours with this easy-going, sociable thirteen-year-old, who had been consumed by a terrible fatigue and could only walk if someone steadied her. He had desperately tried to fit her into a diagnostic category but there had been no evidence of psychosis and barely any evidence of a neurosis. He had then placed all his energies into slotting her into one of the personality disorders. He'd questioned whether it may have been histrionic or emotionally unstable personality disorder but despite his best efforts, he'd had to admit defeat.

"So, am I mad, Doctor?"

When he'd shaken his head, she'd thought he may cry. To justify the hours of his time, he'd decided on a diagnosis of mild post-traumatic stress disorder as a reaction to the initial seizure, possibly compounded by mild anxiety. Although he'd dressed this up in a four-page report, he'd known this was a consequence and not a cause and subsequently returned to patients with more obvious symptoms.

She told Moreover that it was five months. He looked at her with his big brown eyes and he wagged his tail a few times. Within minutes they were both asleep. She had joked with her dad asking him what the difference between her and a koala was?

"I sleep more than a koala!"

Her dad hadn't got it until she'd explained that, of all animals, they sleep the most. He'd made an effort to laugh but it had been difficult. It wasn't really a joke.

When she came to, there was a sparrow on her windowsill. Moreover was already watching it. A car beeped its horn outside and the stupid bird flew into the room. Both girl and dog watched it hop around the room. It wasn't panicking as might be expected but seemed to be exploring the place. She stroked Moreover trying to soothe him to stop him from reacting. The sparrow flew on top of the wardrobe, then down to her books, onto her figurines and for a second only, onto the bottom of the bed. As it hopped about, Lexi began looking at her room as though looking through the eyes of the sparrow. When it disappeared through the open window in one skilful swoop, Lexi sighed. She wasn't sure what this might mean, if anything, but after this she lost her resentment and began making friends of her four walls.

Dexter

There was plenty of time to have another coffee and read the paper. Eleven o'clock, a dragon and this afternoon Ali Hunter wanted a fairy sitting cross-legged on a flower. For Dexter, both were straightforward, both easy-peasy as his youngest son would say. With the studio rebuild lined up for the following weekend, things could only get better.

He was reading about Edgar Welch in the States. Edgar had read online about a restaurant which was harbouring child sex slaves. Armed with a pistol and rifle and thinking himself a hero, he'd burst into the pizzeria and demanded the release of the children. He'd blasted his way into a locked cabinet expecting to free the captives but found an empty cupboard. This, the report continued, was one of a number of conspiracy theories which had arisen online and were dangerously perpetuated without evidence. One person interviewed had told the journalist that the press was covering up the details of what was really going on.

"These situations," he'd asserted "were not conspiracy theories but hidden truths. Ask the President, he knows the truth. They use the term 'conspiracy theory' to distract people or belittle our concerns. Research it yourselves."

That's exactly what Frankie Claxton had said.

He was on the second eye of the dragon when his phone flashed up. He quickly took in the first line: Monies yet to be received.

"Ouch!" The complaint came from Ab Rider—birth name: Richard Partridge—who was over fifty percent into his project to cover both of his muscular arms with tattoo designs.

"Sorry Ab," he said. "This bit is particularly tricky." It wasn't, it was easy-peasy lemon-squeezy. The text had come from Voodoo Tattoo, the people who were doing his rebuild. He had sent the money over yesterday morning. All two-thousand eight-hundred and sixty pounds of it.

Dexter did what he swore never to do—he rushed the last section, a wrap of scales, black outlined with blood red.

"Wow," said Ab Rider, examining his arm in the mirror. "Impressive as ever." But Dexter could see his face slowly changing as he focused on the detail. "Not so sure about his eye, mate."

The Dragon was cross-eyed.

"That sometimes happens with this type of ink." He was positive that Ab picked up on this particular piece of bullshit, but persevered.

"Just a suggestion but if we forget the slit eyes and fill in the entire eye black, I think it would look more menacing. What do you think?"

Ab agreed and was more than happy with the end result. Charging him only one hundred and twenty, Ab Rider, oblivious to the cock-up he had made, left the studio glowing.

Dexter was straight on his phone. The complete text said: *Monies yet to be received. No hurry but required before work can start. Check your emails for details.*

There were two emails—one telling him their bank details and a second one, sent only minutes afterwards, apologising that they had sent the wrong bank account number and sorting code. *Please make the payment now—Ross Gregson of Voodoo Tattoo.*

He checked his account. The monies had been transferred. It was obviously their mistake. Dexter phoned them up. Becoming more exasperated, he put them on loudspeaker and lit a cigarette. He was already pacing the room.

"We thought it strange," they said, "as you said you would send it immediately."

"Once I got your second email, I did it within a few minutes."

"What second email?"

"The one with your new bank details." They got him to read them out.

"Not ours, I'm afraid."

"And Ross Gregson?"

"Never heard of him. I suggest you contact your bank, Mr Jennings."

How he got through the fairy-squatting-on-a-flower he never knew. Usually someone as cute and pale as Ali Hunter would have captured his imagination but he was in another place. He had contacted the bank and they were investigating what may have happened. They would phone him back by the close of business.

He left a voicemail for Dee, his wife, but she was at work and probably hadn't picked it up yet. By four, he was becoming more anxious about what may have happened to his money. He missed Ali's obvious flirting, the touching of his arm, the praise of his work and a possible meeting up to discuss the magnum opus intended for her thighs. He agreed to everything but heard nothing. He ushered her out of the studio, lit another cigarette and waited for the phone to come to life.

It didn't ring until five to five. He had been the victim of a scam.

"What do you mean a victim of a scam? But it's my money? Fucking nigh-on three-thousand quid! And who is this Ross Gregson? Surely he can be traced?"

Apparently, they had recently come across several of these sorts of deceptions. The scammers would use any old name in order to convince the victim that they were legitimate. He was not to worry as there was every chance he would get his money back. The bank had insurance against these sorts of mishaps. However, it would take time. Possibly a couple of weeks. Dexter exploded again, swearing loudly, shaking his fist and concluding the conversation with the understandable question as to who were these evil cunts anyway?

When Dee arrived home, having collected the children from the homes of their respective friends and clearly exhausted from her day as a teaching assistant, Dexter was already on his second bottle of wine.

"Tough day?"

With the children still hovering around, he launched into the tale with the gusto of a storyteller, regularly interjected with the phrase: three-thousand fucking pounds!

"If they're going to get you the cash back, does it really matter?" The calm common sense of his wife set him off again. It was a lot of money.

There was no guarantee they would get it back. Who else could just slip their hands into their accounts whenever they wanted to?

Dee fell asleep almost instantly but Dexter was still raging. He was on his phone, searching scams, hoaxes, frauds, swindles. He hadn't realised there was so much going on. People had lost their homes, some their entire savings. Some poor souls had taken their own lives because they couldn't live with the shame of being deceived.

At three in the morning, he woke up his wife.

"Dee, I've cracked it."

"That's great. Tell me in the morning."

"Remember the second email was signed by one Ross Gregson. I can't find anything online that makes sense. But then I realised. Ross Gregson is an anagram of George Soros."

"Who's that?"

She wished she had never asked. Dexter told her that he was considered by many to be behind all sorts of dodgy things. He was organising a tsunami of deceptions on the world. That's how he had become a multi-billionaire.

"It's been going round and round in my mind and then it hit me."

"But Ross Gregson isn't an anagram of George Soros."

"Near as damn it!" he said, triumphantly.

"If it is him, he's not very good at anagrams, is he?" At that, she turned over and went back to sleep.

Ursula

Whenever Ursula decided to make a chicken casserole, it would conjure up memories of her mother. As a girl she would help her cut onions and dice carrots. By the time she was a teenager her mother had allowed her to make the 'secret' mix of herbs. Of course, there had been nothing secret about it, but her mother had told her that this particular fusion was what made the casserole sing.

"Don't marry that man." These had been among the last words her mother had said to her. Although most of the time she'd slept, occasionally, after her initial confusion on finding she was still alive, she would fight her way through her cognitive fog and come out with something coherent, if unwelcome.

"His name is Robert, mother."

"You can call him what you want but he's no good to you or to anyone. You're giving up the gold for the tinsel."

"Stop that mother."

The gold her mother had been referring to was Ralph Lawrence but as was her tendency, she had been conflating two stories into one. She and Ralph had planned to marry when Ursula was in her early twenties. They had met at college and had fallen for each other before the first term had ended. He had wanted to be a writer, too, but it was not meant to be. Two years after they'd met, Ralph had been working on a farm in the holidays when the gears on a tractor had slipped and he had been impaled on a pallet fork. They'd said he had died instantly but this hadn't been true. The ambulance and fire engine couldn't find the remote farm. Still conscious, his farm mates had been forced to watch the life drain from him. The gold had died a generation ago.

    Robert and Ursula did marry but only after her mother had died—in a parody of the film, they called that year 'four funerals and a wedding'. It occurred to Ursula that people either died too early or too late. Her mother had been preceded by her aunt on her father's side. Aunt Bess had lived her nine miserable decades avoiding fun in all its guises, whereas her best friend from school died from breast cancer aged forty-five. She'd fought for every drop of life she could get. One neighbour wasn't found for three days after he died. Another neighbour had dropped down dead whilst pruning roses. Passing her front garden and the row of roses on a daily basis, Ursula could see exactly where the aneurysm had struck.

Against her mother's advice, she had married Robert anyway. Her best pal, Jorie, had also had reservations but had gone along with it. True, it was a late marriage; both of them were in their forties. But any fool knew there were no rules when it came to love. Robert had been odd jobbing for her. When he'd unblocked her kitchen sink, she'd been so relieved she'd given him a few pounds extra and said she'd owed him a drink.

"How about tonight?" he'd asked, wiping his hands on a tea towel. It had taken her aback but she was a woman of her word and had agreed.

One of the reasons her mother hadn't liked him was that he'd lived in a rented studio flat while Ursula had owned her own place. Her mother could be something of a snob that way. More than once her mother had told her never to trust a man with a moustache. Ursula had pointed out that her dad, who'd had a heart attack when Ursula was ten, had had a moustache.

"Exactly my point", she'd said.

As soon as Ursula got the chicken out, all the animals started showing an interest. She looked down and sighed at the queue which was forming. In ascending order there was Ahmed, Carlo and Desmond. On the other side, the cats. Although tempting, she had learnt not to feed them morsels, because if she forgot the rule, it resulted in total chaos; previous alliances simply went out of the window. Having added the meat component, she slammed the casserole into the oven and announced it was time for a walk.

After a wrestling match of harnesses, leads and coats, they led her through the back door and onto the mud track down to the woods. It was a quiet, calm day. The rain of the last week had finally stopped overnight and it felt like the earth was poised in a state of hushed relief. They arrived at a grassy opening where all three dogs were allowed off their leads. Being slow and ancient, Desmond was already off his lead but she had to watch out for Carlo. He was a pest with other dogs; not nasty but over-playful. Ursula sat on a wooden bench. Over the trees she could see the church steeple. She had to admit to herself that she had not been over there for months. Her poor neglected old mum. When she began improvising a bouquet, the dogs were all around her, surprised at the interruption to the usual routine.

"Not bad, even if I say so myself," she said aloud, Ahmed cocking his head. White buddleia with red campion at its centre and a few strands of yellow pimpernel around the edge.

The grave did look pretty shabby.

"Sorry mother, I really am a hopeless daughter." But she had to be kind to herself; it was only her who went there after all. And because Robert was also buried there, it made any visit to the cemetery difficult. That was her mistake as well. Why in heaven's name had she decided to put him there too? Fortunately, he was on the other side, right in the corner.

She pulled out some weeds, binned the tatty birthday bouquet and fitted her bunch of flowers into the clay pot.

Florence Diane Bird. 1941–2008. Wife and Mother. Rest in Peace.

Not very imaginative words to sum up a person's life. What else could be said? The truth? Could she include such facts such as her mother spoke her mind even if it cut you in two, or that she chain-smoked and died in her sleep but cooked the best chicken casserole?

It was time to get back. Carlo though had wandered off. "Where is the little bugger?" She asked the other two. She shouted his name. Then she made the mistake of looking over to the far corner and there was Robert waving at her, standing there as bold as brass, standing there as if he hadn't been dead for six years.

She urgently busied herself with the dogs but when she looked up again, he was still there; the bastard was still waving to her.

The house smelt divine when she burst through the door. The dogs, picking up their owner's vibe, were subdued and unusually obedient. Her eyes were moist with her tears when she went straight to the sherry bottle. Her coat still on, she slumped down in her chair, five animals watching her, wondering what had happened.

Half a bottle of sherry later she was still wondering herself.

Matthew

Matthew woke up at a few minutes past ten. He had to check the clock a couple of times before he accepted the truth: he had slept for twelve hours. This was extraordinary. His usual time of waking was seven, seven-thirty at the latest.
What did it mean?

He swung his legs out of bed and sat there checking that this was definitely his body and everything was in the right place. In fact, he concluded he felt absolutely tiptop! He made a cup of tea about three hours later than usual, sat in his favourite chair and opened up the Guardian. Protests were still going on in the USA. People had taken to the streets because Donald Trump, the six-times bankrupt businessman with the orange hair, was now installed in the White House. It would be interesting to see how that panned out.

He was more interested though in an article he was reading on Leonard Cohen, who had died some months before. He used to sing Famous Blue Raincoat to Joy, or try to. It was so bad it always made her laugh. His singing voice was weak and had a tremor to it. She would have to shut him up with a kiss on his mouth.

"Thank you, Leonard," she would say.

Ever since he'd posted the dog collar to the bishop, Matthew had experienced the sort of renaissance he had craved for many years. Unrestricted by the obligations of filling-in wherever there was the need, he'd felt a wonderful liberty. But more than that, the peace of being godless and faithless had unleashed a new faculty in his head. He had been caught up with this endless struggle with a god who'd never answered and who'd remained silent even in the face of hatred or harm. It had been like arguing with a chair, except at least a chair had its uses.

Within a few days of posting the collar, he had been surprised to receive a note back from the bishop. It too had been written on a dog collar. It too was left unsigned. It had simply said: *Make no bones, he will find you—he knows where you live!*

One of the first things he did was put one box of books away—ecclesiastical texts and the like—and bring out another box of books, which had laid there for decades, forgotten and gathering dust. He'd rediscovered the brutal world of Zola and the fatalistic world of Hardy, the swoons of Lawrence and the political thrillers of Graham Greene. He'd told Fiona it was like rediscovering a lost gang of friends who had been living under his stairs all the time.

"Like Harry Potter."

"Harry who?"

"You know, Harry Potter, the wizard. He lived under the stairs as well."

"Yes," he said, struggling to see the link. "Just like Harry Potter."

He made himself some scrambled eggs on toast, chuckling to himself as to whether this was a late breakfast or an early lunch. After eating, he read a few stories from Katherine Mansfield's collection. An hour later, he woke up again.

"Bloody hell! I've got some sort of sleeping sickness!"

He threw on his coat and left his house as quickly as he could, lest he fall asleep again.

It was a release to find himself outside. The incessant rain of the last few weeks was having a break. The island was bathed in the peculiar orangey light that sometimes spilled in from the South West. On a whim, he decided to climb the hill to the top.

This proved quite a challenge and he had to stop several times to catch his breath. There was no doubt that his asthma was getting progressively worse. It didn't stop him from doing stuff and was never as bad as it had been when he was a child, but it was definitely on the ascendency. Folklore had it that it came in seven-year cycles which, in this case, was actually right in the middle of his ninth cycle.

  Finally at the top, he scanned the horizon. It never lost that wow! moment. To the west, you could trace the beach, rising onto the orange hills of Charmouth. Drop into West Bay, climb Golden Cap and enter Devon, and it was rumoured that on a good day, you could see the beach in Torquay. To the east, the eyes leapt over the town, followed Weymouth Sands, soared over the White Nothe, onto Durdle Door, into Lulworth and coming finally to St Aldhelm's head. That's a view of a hundred miles or more. He walked on.

  He took the footpath which hugged the cliff edge. In some places, you had to be on high alert. One moment's lapse and you would be taking an unexpected long dive into the noisy sea below. It was starting to get dark already, but he was determined to walk further. He knew it made no sense to go on — he would have to turn back at some point. But he didn't.

He arrived at Portland Bill around midnight. He could hardly see his hand in front of his face, but when he looked up there was the whole universe, floating above him.

"I think I've made a terrible mistake," he told some cows in a field he was passing. If he'd had the sense to bring his phone, he could call a taxi but he could sense defiance in himself; he wanted to be out there. He was cold, he was hungry but he was where he wanted to be; a little old man contemplating the indifferent heavens. He comforted himself with the thought that, but for his contemplation, the universe didn't even know it existed.

"So, I think I'm having the last laugh!"

He settled down in a bus shelter and fell into a drowsy, prickly sleep. He must have been there for a few hours when he was shaken awake by his wife, Joy—or that's what it felt like.

"Come on old man. Time to go home."

He thought it was sensible to take the road. About a mile along a car pulled up beside him.

"You're an early riser, grandad. Want a lift?"

"I think I do."

"Goodness me! You're a bit on the cold side," said the driver, helping him get into the passenger's seat. "Where can I take you too?"

When they pulled up outside the house, the sun peering over the horizon, Fiona was at the garden gate.

"Matthew Price, where in heaven have you been?" He remembered his mother saying those exact same words, but he was too tired to tell her. "I was about to call the police and coast guard and whoever else you call when someone goes missing. Where have you been?"

"I went for a walk," he whispered.

Tia

Somebody had grassed Tia up. An anonymous letter had been sent to the Benefits Office informing them that she had been doing a part-time job in a local cafe for over six months. Tia thought it odd that when she wanted to get an answer from them, they took their time; they lost letters or asked endlessly for more information. When, however, they thought someone had not disclosed the correct details or were trying to cheat the system, they came down on you like a ton of bricks. The letter informed her that, if she had been working and this had not been declared, she was not only liable to repay the amount in full but could also be guilty of a criminal offence.

The person who interviewed her was about her own age. He was dressed in a shirt and tie but wore it like a teenager at a wedding. Mr Jarvis adopted a casual manner with her and was clearly enjoying having the upper hand. As she wasn't aware how much information had been passed to them, she decided to play it straight. It was only two hours every Friday. Cash in hand.

"And you didn't think to make this known to us?"

"It was such a small amount, I thought it didn't matter. Can't you earn so much before you have to declare it?"

"I'm afraid," he said, making no attempt to hide his smirk, "that's one of the myths that some of our claimants like to perpetuate."

They worked out that she had been overpaid by £260.

"How do you propose to clear this debt?" He could see she had no idea. "Okay, I've just got to go and have a word with my supervisor. I'll be right back."

She was suddenly alone in the office. It wasn't much of an office, more like a glass cubicle carved out of a real office. A poster with a family was smiling back at her: *Working together for the Benefit of the Community*. In the adjoining cubicles, she could hear other people talking through their problems. She thought she heard someone crying, then a man started shouting. Apparently, everyone who worked there were total and utter wankers.

She picked her book from her bag. This was her latest find. *Mindfulness: 25 ways to live in the moment through Art* by Christophe Andre.

The shop assistant had thanked her for buying it. "It's been in the bargain basket for well over a year."

Tia couldn't understand; it was a little hidden treasure as far as she was concerned. The paintings alone were marvellous but the accompanying commentary relating them to mindfulness was fascinating. She had hardly ever thought about mindfulness before, but here it was celebrated as the means to remain authentically in the here and now. She went about life in a state of accepting life as best she could, regardless of what was thrown at her. This took it to a new level, she thought, seeing the mind not so much as part of you but somehow separate, something you could use like you would use a tool.

"Right, Miss Hearn, I have some good news. We have decided not to press for criminal proceedings. So, it is merely a question of getting the money back. You have a choice to pay it in a lump sum or £130 a month for two months or £86.67 a month over three months. Which would you prefer?"

"Ideally, spread out over the six months as it took me that long to earn it?" Jarvis looked disappointed. "I suppose over the three months then," she offered.

Once out of the office, she sat down on a bench overlooking the park. She needed a minute to reflect on what had just occurred. She rolled one of her famous matchstick cigarettes. She did the sums in her head. Basically, she was £30 short every week until the beginning of August.

"Fuck."

It was going to be difficult, maybe impossible, but it was what it was. She had a second cigarette and pulled her book out of the bag. Opening it randomly she came across a quote by Swami Prajnanpad, whoever he was. *Accept ... there is nothing else.*

"Easy for him to say. I bet Mr Prajnanpad wasn't on benefits."

She was busy making the children their dinner — cheesy beans on toast — when there was an unexpected knock on the door.

"See who it is, Nara!"

"It's Mr Forecourt or something like that."

"Nara, keep an eye on Kojo."

She knew exactly who it was. The landlord's son, Mr Forshaw who was nick-named Foreskin to her friends. Previously, his father would do the rounds, but he was around seventy now and was so heavy he struggled to walk properly. If she was behind with the rent, he would make allowances for her. Once, if she could have reached his face, she would have actually kissed him when he let her off a whole month's rent. In stepped his youngest son, who was a totally different animal. She had seen him press his fist against Pete's face when he had fallen behind.

"I have a queue of people," he had told him through gritted teeth, "just lining up to get into this place." Pete had almost shat himself and emptied out everything in his pockets. A fiver and a few coins.

"I wasn't expecting you until tomorrow."

"Last day of the month or the first day of the month, does it make much difference?"

"Well, to me, yes, it does."

"Whatever," he said, rolling his eyes. "It's the usual month's rent plus the outstanding £80 you owe."

"Your dad said I could pay that out of my Christmas bonus and then over the course of next year."

"Please don't go phoning up my dad behind my back. I'm responsible for this side of things now."

"As far as I am concerned, he's still my landlord."

"Technically, yes. Practically, no. You know Tia, there are ways and means."

"What do you mean by that?"

He raised his hand and, for a second, she thought he might slap her. But, in a way which confused her, he left his hand hanging in the air. Then he allowed it to drop and touched her breast.

"You have just reduced your debt right there. It's as easy as that, Tia." Before she could make sense of what had happened, he turned on his heels and was gone.

CHAPTER 3
October 2017

Theresa May now leads a minority government, the reverse of her intention.

The right wing of the Tory Party wants the UK to become a completely independent trading nation free of Europe.

The press is still discussing Jacob Rees-Mogg's comments that food banks are an 'uplifting' sign of a compassionate country.

Fourth hottest October since records began.

Jon

Jon Fox couldn't believe how he was being treated. He felt like a wayward schoolboy sitting outside the headmaster's office — and it wasn't even the Head of Department's Office. He was sitting on a plastic chair outside her stooge's office, Ian Tait, the so-called Associate Head.

The email had said ten o'clock sharp and here he was twenty minutes later flicking through the news for the third time. Every paper was obsessed with Article 50 of the Treaty on European Union and the endless stream of issues that entailed. One headline stated that the United Kingdom would become independent again within a year. Strange, Jon thought, I didn't know we weren't independent. Must have missed something.

"Ah, Jon, Jon, Jon, so sorry to keep you waiting. You know how it is." Tait was suddenly standing in front of him, holding the door open and grinning his bogus smile.

"Can we get a move on? I've got a shitload of papers to mark by the time I start my class later."

"You must admit things are much easier since we've gone completely electronic? So technically it's no longer a shitload of papers," he said, pausing and pretending to think of a suitable alternative. "Maybe, a click-load of digits?"

It was obvious Tait was trying to pass off as original something he had said before. To Jon, it merely confirmed that the man was a complete imbecile.

"So, what's this about?"

Tait took this as a cue to launch into a monologue describing the changes ahead, the need for the university to adapt and for individual lecturers to rise to the inevitable demands of the current academia.

Jon hadn't a clue where this gobbledygook was leading but noted that some phrases came straight out of the university's prospectus.

"My apologies, Ian," Jon finally interjected. "I can't quite see what this has to do with me. Could we get down to specifics?"

"Specifics, of course." But off he went again on his diatribe of self-important nonsense. Jon couldn't stop himself from looking at his watch. This seemed to sober the man up. He cleared his throat and announced with a plastic smirk that the Critical Thinking module had to be curtailed.

"Curtailed?"

"Not so much curtailed as dropped."

It was Jon's turn to laugh. "Now I know you're wasting my time, Ian. The Critical Thinking Course has been the bedrock of all our courses. As you well know, it is envied across the academic world."

"When this current course concludes, we are pulling the plug on it. The essential elements of the course will be assimilated into other programmes."

"So, you're expecting me to rush from one programme to another delivering in a totally haphazard and random way?"

"That's the thing, Jon, you won't be teaching any of it."

Ladies and Gentlemen, we suddenly have the truth! He was being marginalised. He was being side-lined by the likes of this wretched sycophant.

"Mr Tait, you are completely out of your depth. How long have you been here in the university? 12 short months?"

"Two years actually."

"I've been here ten times that, you pathetic upstart. I know how this place ticks. I know what our students need. You can't just come along and trash it all for no good reason. Anyway, tell me what in this great plan were you intending to do with me?"

It was difficult to find any trace of a grin on Tait's face now. Whilst Jon Fox was getting louder, he was getting quieter. Tait kept looking at the phone: Security was 376. Or was it 367? But he hadn't delivered the final punch and it would be professionally embarrassing if he came out of this interview knowing that another one would have to be convened almost immediately.

"You would basically," he blurted out, "become an assistant lecturer filling in wherever you are required."

"You must know, the union wouldn't allow that. Just relocate me into another department. Standard practice."

"None want you, Jon. To be frank, the Critical Thinking module was originally put together to get you out of the way. You're not the most popular of people in these halls, and there are these allegations about fraternising with our female students."

"All withdrawn or unproven," he lit up a cigarette and could see that Tait wanted to chastise him but when Jon glowered at him, he thought better of it.

"True, all withdrawn or unproven," confirmed Tait, who had visibly run of steam.

"I've fucking had enough of this," said Jon, jumping to his feet. He stubbed the newly-lit cigarette out on his table. "You've picked the wrong person to pick a fight with."

He found himself on a bench in the avenue of trees which skirted the road to the main reception door. He was so mad; he couldn't focus on anything and yet some phrases kept exploding in his head: None want you—fucking assistant lecturer—put together to get me out of the way. What the fuck?

Through the battlefield of colliding thoughts, he tried to think what he must do. Phone Lynda? But things were not good between them. Ever since he'd discovered that she had been having an affair with Pratt the Twat, life had become strained, every interaction becoming either clipped, over self-conscious or smarmy. When he had confronted her, she'd produced a list of how many 'liaisons' he'd had with his students or the younger lecturers. It was a long list, and some, she delighted in telling him, were of a similar age to Victoria, his own daughter.

To add insult to injury, she'd verbalised a list of her own which had included a colleague, a handful of his club friends and two women, separately and, on occasions, together.

He'd ranted and protested that the list was somehow not equal. He'd smashed a bottle of red wine against the wall to emphasise his disgust, but in the end, he'd had to concede that the marriage was a charade. When they had got drunk later though and both had become reflective, it had been quite obvious that neither had wanted to give up their habits: nor their house, their holidays, their cars, or their way of life. They had decided not to go for the domestic equivalent of Article 50 but to continue and hoist the flag of convenience into place.

No, he would speak to her later about it but first things first, he needed to get hold of Ted Jenkins, his inept union representative.

He was just about to tap his name into his phone, when a message beat him to it. No text, but a picture of him lying on a hotel bed completely naked, looking away but clearly happy with himself, penis still swollen with a sad tear dripping down his stem.

Lexi

The family had decided to go to the beach. The weather was beautiful for this time of the year, the sands were tourist-free, the air was fresh but warm and the sky was an endless blue with wisps of cloud feathering the horizon.

Lexi couldn't go. No doubt she was becoming stronger. She could make it downstairs without help, and into the garden on good days, but these remained odd days in an eternal morass of generic fatigue and arbitrary pain. An excursion to the beach was beyond her reach. She had to watch her family pack up for the day and walk down to the shore.

From her window, she watched them disappear onto the pathway to the beach and then reappear as they skirted the park. She couldn't see them on the beach but Harry and Sara had promised her that they would walk out on the cobb and wave to her from the end. She had her binoculars ready.

Hiya Fuckwit. How the devil are you? I'm an orphan for the day, how about you? Rayn's texts were always funny and jam-packed with fucks and shits.

Guess what? I'm an orphan too! Fancy coming over?

On my way!

Lexi loved seeing Rayn. She was a real tonic. She hardly took any notice of her illness and could chat for hours without drawing breath. Her dad called Rayn a phenomenon of nature.

Over the months since Lexi had become ill, most of her friends had drifted away. In the first month, it had been chaos; half the school had trooped around. She had been inundated with cards, chocolates and grapes. Her class had put together a video in which they took turns to give their good wishes. Her former best mate, Freya Bankwell had come around every day for a month.

When people began to realise that she wasn't getting better quickly and that she hadn't been given a diagnosis, a change snuck in, as elusive as the illness itself. Visits had dropped off so suddenly that it was as if they had discovered that she had a terrible virus, highly contagious, for which there was no treatment. Rumours and conjectures had crept in to fill the vacuum. Was it all in her mind? Was it a fabricated illness? Was it a cop-out, an opt-out or an excuse? Perhaps her illness wasn't an unfortunate blow but a matter of choice.

While she waited for Rayn to walk from Uplyme, she put on some music. She was really into Sia at this time. It took her somewhere she wanted to be. Hearing her words seemed to brutally describe her.

There's a scream inside me that we all try to hide. When Sia sang the words *I'll shout it out like a bird set free*, Lexi felt overcome with emotion, every time. Sometimes she would clench her fists. She would allow tears to run down her face. When the lyrics of the next song came on, it was almost unbearable for her. *I put my armour on. I'll show you that I am unstoppable.*

Her friends had dwindled to three. Rayn, of course, and Carla and Molly popped in once a week. Maybe, she could count Jacob. He didn't come round that often but it was at least regular, once every month. The visits were short, the conversation limited and awkward, but he had kissed her on the cheek when he came to say goodbye, which was interesting.

She often wondered why these three remained and the others had fled. Freya texted every now and then, but if invited over, she made a plethora of excuses as to why she couldn't visit. She had last come over during the summer holidays. Granted she had arrived with a gift. Lexi had joked that she hoped it was roller skates. When it had been another pair of slippers, the joke had fallen flat. But she had read Freya's face; she hadn't wanted to be there. Lexi had deduced that the common denominators of the three who remained were that they were quirky and accepting of her situation rather than incessantly trying to find evidence of improvements or seek explanations for what had happened to her.

Lexi could hear Rayn letting herself in and leaping up the stairs two at a time. Lexi was sitting on the seat by the window, ready for her dramatic entry. The door swung open wide and there was Rayn doing her tra-la!

"And I do not come empty-handed, my friend."

She produced a packet of cigarettes and a small bottle of gin. Lexi clapped her hands. Rayn needed no further encouragement. She turned up the sounds, opened the windows and helped Lexi out of the chair.

Gin in their mugs and smoking out of the window, they started talking about anything that came into their minds. Michael Shorton had been picked up shoplifting. Amy was pregnant—no surprise there. One of the teachers, a Mr Hudson, had slipped a disc when laying into one of the kids and nobody knew whether he was off sick or suspended or both.

"Everything alright with you?" Lexi found that Rayn could talk about everyone and everything except for herself.

"All good, Lexi."

"Don't give me: all good, Lexi. Tell me, how you are."

"All I know is that this gin is fucking awful, isn't it," she said making a face. "Next time I'll steal some tonic as well."

It was true, the neat gin was lethal but Lexi chose not to respond. She allowed them to lapse into an unusual silence.

"Fucking shit, if you really want to know."

"I do really want to know. What's going on Rayn?"

"Nothing really, just a bit of bother at school."

Lexi waited.

"Some girls seem to have a problem with me."

"Not like you to let that worry you?"

"Fucking Facebook," she said, lighting another cigarette. "These bitches manage to find something to say about me most days. Today for example, it's my hair. What's wrong with purple?"

"Nothing, it's cool."

This brought tears into her eyes and she drew Lexi towards her for a hug.

"Who are the girls? Our year?"

"Yep, sure are. The leader is that old friend of yours."

"Freya?"

"She turned out to be one almighty cunt, I'm afraid."

Lexi wasn't shocked to find out that her old bestie was capable of being a cunt. She had been aware of a catty side to her friend. Freya had a sort of pretence to her and was overly concerned with her appearance.

"Who are those idiots waving like crazy on the cobb?"

"Ha! That's Harry and Sara. Wave back!"

"If only they knew their sister was a bit pissed and smoking."

As soon as Rayn left, Lexi texted Freya. She held the phone in her hand and thought about what she wanted to say. It would be as easy as it would be lame to tell her to leave Rayn alone. Sia's words came to the rescue. They were slightly out of context and obscure but that's exactly what she wanted. So, just before she deleted Freya's contact from her phone, she wrote: *I've got a thick skin and an elastic heart. Leave Rayn alone—never contact me again*

Dexter

It was Bill Walker's birthday and the usual suspects turned out for the celebration in the Rendezvous. The harbour-side venue with its decorative lighting and pumping music appeared to hold the promise of a good night, but except perhaps for Friday and Saturday nights, the place was forgotten and the dance floor remained empty. If they were lucky, they might bump into a hen gang, but Thursday nights were usually mundane and uneventful.

Apart from the two serving behind the bar, the only women there were with partners. Every time it was their round, whether married or not, in a relationship or not, every last man instigated a chat-up line with them and every last man thought they had a chance of something spicier than a Gingerbread Manhattan.

Dexter was no different to the rest. He knew one of the bar staff from school. He mistook this as an advantage, but Ellie Baker was a connoisseur at feigning interest whilst hiding the intensity of her boredom. When he reached for her hand Ellie, with the practised smile of a physician giving bad news, asked how his kids were. He left the bar grinning to himself, believing he was way in front of the others.

Dexter had put the last few months to good use. He hadn't done that well at school and couldn't even remember if he had two GCSEs or three, but since Frankie Claxton had visited his studio almost a year ago, he had discovered an innate ability to study, to recover facts and to search out truths previously concealed from him.

The quest had had an overwhelming effect. In some mysterious way, his research had made him feel alive, important, bigger than himself. He'd found that not only was he blessed with tattooing skills unparalleled on the south coast, he was also in a prime position to preach the word to others. When the customer was prone, often apprehensive, he was in an ideal position to tell them about the true nature of reality. He'd recognised he was a novice and standing at the beginning but this was not daunting; it was exciting. As feathers or owls or tigers emerged from the skin of his patrons, he'd try out ideas which he had recently uncovered.

His latest nugget of knowledge was around the attack on the twin towers in 2001. It was so obvious that the American government had planned it themselves in order to justify the invasions of Afghanistan and Iraq. It annoyed him that he hadn't spotted it before. He'd been amazed at how many people had agreed with him. Typical of Dee, she had remained a misbeliever. He had been sorry to call her a fucking moron in front of the boys, but for God's sake, why couldn't she see what was clearly self-evident?

After six rounds of lager, it was onto the cocktails: buy one get one free. They all knew this was a mistake but couldn't resist the euphoria of being lads out together. Beneath the customary chatter about women, work and cars, the subject they all hated and loved was lingering like a shadow waiting to be invited in.

Everyone avoided it until about half ten, then Phil Redstone, who enjoyed a reputation of being a total shit-stirrer, called it out. At last, Britain was leaving Europe. The subject caused such agitation, but it allowed Dexter an opportunity to air his own views. Brexit was the result of both American and Russian interference—splitting the European Union was obviously in their best interests, although for very different reasons. Of late, he had noticed some rolled their eyes when he'd started to explain or expose some palpable facts. Annoying though this was, he'd had to accept that misbelievers were still in the majority.

At one point, Ellie had to come over to ask them to keep their voices down. Wanting to impress her with their maturity, they managed to do so for about ten minutes. The three of them who believed that Europe was a good thing were putting up a good fight against the five who disagreed.

"You actually believe," said Redstone, "that you want to continue being a slave state?" If we didn't get out, it was a given that they would lose their jobs to the seventy million Turks itching to come to the UK.

Nick Grainger glugged his beer down and left without so much as a goodbye or a happy birthday to the birthday boy.

That left the two of them, Paul Cross and Bernie Chivers, hostages to a debate they were undoubtedly losing. Cross was trying to laugh it off and be philosophical but Bernie was boiling over.

Seeing he was winning the argument hands down, Redstone played his trump card. Was it true then, Mr Chivers, you want to see the NHS dismantled and sold off to the private sector? Chivers was a paramedic and couldn't contain himself anymore. He flew across the table. Both men ended up on the ground, not so much fighting as hugging with attitude. Ellie and her colleague were straight on them, screaming for them to get out or the police would be called.

The group ended outside in pairs or groups of three. All were surprised that their evening had been so suddenly curtailed and there they were: outside in the cold autumn night.

Dexter found himself consoling Chivers. Dexter reminded him that he should know what Redstone was like. Chivers cursed him more than a few times and swore never to go near that wanker again. As they walked the path alongside the harbour, Dexter, sobering up after the adrenaline rush, tried to cheer up his mate with a little education.

"It's so hard to really make sense of what is going on in the world at the moment. It's absolutely deliberate though. We're all being controlled, you know, controlled and manipulated, the entire world is being dragged into debt. What do you think the national debt is?" As yet, Chivers wasn't taking much notice. "I'll tell you. It's more than one thousand seven hundred billion. Billion! Ask yourself then, where exactly are we borrowing this from?"

"I couldn't care a flying fuck, to be honest. Will you shut up peddling these bloody stupid ideas! It won't be long before you'll be saying is the earth is flat."

"Well, now you bring that up …"

The next thing Dexter recalled was falling through the air and plunging into the dark water of the harbour. In the morning, Dee asked him why his clothes were wringing wet.

"Did you lads go for a midnight dip?"

"Something like that," he whispered.

Ursula

This would be her fifth book fayre at the Corn Exchange. Ursula had tried to attend every one of them but had missed a few; notably, thanks to Robert, the 2010 fayre.

This year's fayre promised to be the most successful so far. People were anticipating it this year. Richard Bass had publicised it properly for the first time — the usual stamp-size advert in the local paper and a few pink posters sellotaped to telegraph poles could hardly be deemed adequate. The rumour that he may be dispensed with had proven to be a wonderful motivation. This year he had involved local businesses, arranged an interview with the County radio station and, shock of shocks, started a Facebook page.

And this time around, Ursula had six books to present on her stall. In 2010 she'd only had two: her first novel, *The Mindless Clock* and the first collection of her short stories.

She was one of the first to arrive at the Exchange. Her neighbour, Maisie, was looking after her menagerie for the day. She would have preferred to use her closest friend, Jorie, but she was away visiting family. Maisie did her best but with their varying walking habits and dietary foibles, this was no small feat and her reward, a bottle of Prosecco and a box of Friars hand-made chocolates, would be well deserved.

"I think you have the prime spot, Ursula."

It was Greg Andrews. Ursula was immediately suspicious. Wherever she was, he seemed to make an unwelcome appearance. Granted, he had every right to be there: he was an aspiring author and had a relatively successful graphic novel under his belt. Did that mean he always had to strike up a conversation with her? He picked up her latest novel from the stand she had just assembled and started flicking through it.

"You have been busy. What's this one all about?"

"A summary is on the back," she snapped.

"A fall from the world of politics," he read, "leads to a man discovering that the best things in life are free. Sounds fascinating."

She wanted to retort that it sounded utter claptrap the way he'd read it aloud. She practically tore it from him and returned it to its place. Ignoring her attitude, he asked her if he could buy a copy.

"You really don't have to, you know."

"No, I want to. It's my sort of thing."

Reluctantly, she sold it to him. For a moment, she thought about giving it to him at cost price but she charged him the full ten pounds. After all, self-publishing, or self-printing as Robert had mocked her, wasn't cheap.

Richard appeared with a latte for her. He spent some respectful moments looking over her display before congratulating her.

"You all set for the ten o'clock opening?"

"Yes, but not sure they are."

Several other authors were struggling with tables which refused to unfold, or with displays which, despite their best efforts, looked woefully amateur. Greg looked at his watch, fifteen minutes to zero hour, and hurried off to offer his help.

Ursula sat on her stool, sipping her coffee. Despite herself, her mind kept returning to 2010, the year before Robert had died.

Robert had scoffed at her the year before but hadn't raised an objection to her attending. But by 2010, he had grown in confidence. He'd started talking about *his* house and *his* car, even though he had not contributed a penny to either. When he'd actively started nagging her to place the deeds into joint ownership and to change her will, she'd had to admit to herself that her mother had been right about Robert. In fact, as soon as he'd moved in after their registry office wedding, he'd begun the slow transformation from kind and quirky to selfish and overbearing.

They'd had a terrible row the night before the book fayre. He'd been drunk, as usual, on strong cider and this had put him into a particularly belligerent mood. He'd stood in the middle of the lounge, waving his hands about and insulting her with whatever words arrived in his head. He mocked her as a fake; that she was pretending to be someone she wasn't.

"A writer! A writer! Don't make me laugh. You can hardly string two words together!"

She'd said nothing as he'd taken out one of her books which had been boxed up ready for the fayre. He'd randomly opened it and read out a sentence in a pseudo-posh voice. It hadn't helped that Rossetti, her Lakeland terrier, had kept intervening on her behalf, snapping at his heels and barking.

"Christine was well aware she was lying to herself but, if any situation demanded it, this was undoubtedly it. " He'd struggled on the word *undoubtedly* but this hadn't stopped him falling into a hearty belly laugh at her expense. "What a fucking load of fucking crap!" He'd thrown it to the floor, stamping on it with theatrical emphasis.

In the morning, she'd woken up hours before the alarm. Robert had been comatose beside her, snoring like an old horse. As she'd crept downstairs, she'd become aware of a dreadful smell. She'd been about to chastise one of the dogs when she'd spotted its source. Robert had opened up her box of books and had shat and pissed on them. Watched by a mystified Rossetti and a sad Desmond, she'd sunk to the floor and wept. If only this had been the lowest point, maybe she could have picked herself up, but worse was to come.

She sold more copies this year than she had in all the other fayres put together. Her purse had never held three-hundred pounds before.

"I can see you have had a successful fayre, Ursula."

It was Greg again. Why couldn't he leave her alone? Out of politeness, she asked him how he had done.

"Not bad, but not good either. People still think graphic novels are just for kids." She was one of those people. "Want a hand packing up?"

"No, thank you. I know where everything goes and how it fits in together."

"Okay, see you at the next fayre then?"

"Most probably."

The dogs greeted her as if she had been gone for months on a special mission to Mars. Maisie had clearly had enough of them and, loaded with her gifts, she made her excuses and headed home almost immediately. Once she had fed and walked them, Ursula spread her winnings on the kitchen table.

"It may be a takeaway tonight," she informed the animals. It was then, at that exact moment, that a new story presented itself like a revelation. Everything at once, the entire thing. She ordered her Lamb Ceylon and waited in her lounge with the full knowledge that she was an author of a truly amazing book. All she had to do was write the first word.

Matthew

Entering the living room, the curtains still drawn, Fiona found Matthew sitting in his favourite chair, absentmindedly stroking the cat on his lap. In her naturally practical way, she strode across the room, pulled the curtains apart and opened a window.

"What's the meaning of this, Mr Price?"

"I'm not sure, my dear," he said, sluggishly as if coming round from a trance, "I plumped down here an hour ago and couldn't find a good enough reason to move."

Fiona put her hands on her hips and studied him for a minute.

"Right, Matthew, this is what's going to happen. You're going to get into some clothes and we're going out for the day."

"How about the cleaning and all that?"

"The cleaning and all that can wait. I think you need to get out and breathe some fresh air. You look like you've been sleeping under a stone all night."

Less than half an hour later, they were in her old Saab, which she had got at a knock-down price when the company went bankrupt.

"Where are we going?"

"I'm thinking Dorchester."

"Why Dorchester? I haven't been there these last ten years."

"Well, good reason to go now then, isn't it? As you have been rambling on about Hardy for weeks, I thought we could visit his grave at Stinsford. Have you ever been?"

"Not at all."

"So, you've lived here all your life just ten miles away and you have never visited?"

"I suppose there were always more important things to do."

"You know, it's only his heart which is buried there."

"Where's the rest of him?"

"Westminster Abbey, I think."

"Strange."

They drew up outside the church.

"I'm not going in, Fiona."

"Thought you were free of it all now?"

"I want it to stay that way, thank you very much."

Fiona rolled her eyes. "But surely, by not going in, you're acknowledging his presence. Or at least his influence over you?"

"True, true. I'm still not going in."

She helped him out of the car and they slowly made their way into the church grounds. There was something about the modest graveyard which seemed to hold back the world outside of it. The dead had a sanctuary of trees which framed their own stretch of sky and provided an unhindered asylum for birds.

"Big grave for his little heart. And look, his mother's name was Jemima. That's nice. "The oldest of Job's daughters."

"Is that right?"

"Come on, let's sit a minute."

They allowed themselves to sink into the silence of the place. A robin alighted on the headstone of the poet laureate, Cecil Day-Lewis.

"It was a day like today. Joy died on a day like today. Have I ever told you about that?"

"No, you never have."

"Up to the point of the accident, it was a great day. We opened the garden of the vicarage up to whoever wanted to come. Joy was an avid gardener and spent hours tending to her flowers. She loved it and tasked herself with trying to achieve a floral display for each season of the year. Even winter."

"Did you give her a hand?"

"Not a chance," chuckled Matthew. "Joy called me a 'slash and burn' gardener, so the closest

I got to a plant was the bonfire. The usual troops arrived. The locals were very loyal. They were always fund-raising for something or other. But family came as well. My brother, Jack, and my sister, Margaret, both came along with their kids. I lit the barbeque, opened some wine and all was well in the world. We even had a band. Oh, yes, a band. Some of the village teenagers had formed a band called the Impossible Possibles. They weren't that bad, not exactly the Beetles, but not bad." He was becoming tearful and took a deep breath.

She patted his leg lightly.

"Matthew, you don't have to tell me any more."

"Joy was in her element. She looked adorable. She was wearing this peach-coloured dress with a scarf of sorts, no idea what you would call it, draping her on both sides. A thing of beauty is a joy forever. I would always be saying that to her. You know, from the poem by Keates."

"I know," Fiona said, smiling.

"Then Jack's youngest son, Ben, made his entrance. We heard him coming before we saw him. He had passed his test only the month before. He bought himself a Mazda of some sort and zoomed up the engine. Jack told me the insurance was almost as much as the car. Anyway, the afternoon progressed nicely and we all had a super time. We were gathering outside the gate, saying our goodbyes, when Ben roared up in his car as he was giving one of the guests a lift to the station. He opened the door for the passenger and came round to wish us a farewell. In one moment, he turned and jumped in the car wanting to make an impressive getaway. Unfortunately, Joy's drape got caught in the car door. It happened so quickly. Ben revved up and stormed away. I remember Joy being suddenly pulled towards the car. Her head caught the side, the drape tore off and she was left lying there on the pavement."

They gave each other some time for the tears to flow. She hugged the old man to her until he leant back.

"At once, I knew she was gone. Everyone screamed, or fussed, or cried but I knew in that split second that all was lost, that Joy was no more."

Fiona took Matthew into town for a cream tea. Whilst there, they saw a notice in the window that there was a book fayre that day, just across the road from them. Determined to take his mind off things, she suggested going in. His face lit up when he saw the large number of book stalls lining both sides of the hall. Fiona had to stop him from buying every book that drew his attention.

"You'll never read that many." But after she was talking to a seller who had actually bought her first house from her, she found him again buying two more from a local author, Ursula Bird.

"Fiona, you must meet Ursula. Look at all her work. Most impressive. And here," he said, holding up a copy of *The Mindless Clock*, "is the story of a man falling out with God. How spooky is that?"

It wasn't until the car crossed the sole causeway which served the island that Fiona asked him a question which had been troubling her all afternoon.

"Matthew, was that what made you give it up?"

He knew precisely what she meant. "I wouldn't have said that at the time, but now I would say that it was the start," he said with a smile, lightly thumping the pile of books sitting on his lap. "Let us say, a seed of doubt was firmly planted."

Tia

Tia met Louise Hill at the food bank. After a lean Christmas, her GP had signed the referral form; the entry ticket required before access was permitted. Dr Armstrong had been irritated with having to complete it, not with Tia but with the government.

"What are we, the fifth or sixth richest economy in the world? And we have thousands of food banks? Don't get me started on what that Rees-Mogg character said about food banks."

Tia had had no intention of getting her started on anything. Under the section where the doctor had needed to specify the reasons for the referral, she'd read her answer aloud as she'd written. "Because the government has neglected its basic duty to feed and shelter its citizens."

"I'm not being funny, Dr Armstrong, but will they accept that as a reason?"

"Oh, they're used to me. To be honest, I don't think anyone reads them. I could probably write any old rubbish and they would accept it."

Unlike Tia, Louise had no problem using the food bank or receiving any other freebies she could get her hands on. As far as Louise was concerned it was her born right to grab her slice of the cake, however big or small it was.

Louise both fascinated and terrified Tia. If they went into a shop, invariably Louise would come out with a little extra something she had sneaked into her bag or wedged into her coat. When Tia had told her she should be careful, Louise shrugged it off.

"No one is interested, Tia. We're down with the vermin. The police aren't interested and social services don't give a shit. Benefits are shit and getting shittier. It's done on purpose to get us to fend for ourselves. That's all I'm doing."

Tia could see what her friend meant. Louise appeared to be as resilient as she was fragile and wishy-washy.

One night when Tia had hit a low point and the children had been in bed, she'd texted Louise in desperation. Within half an hour Louise had knocked at the door with a bottle of wine and a huge bag of mini cakes; both stolen. Louise had told—not asked—her ex to come and look after their child, Dalton, for a couple of hours while she went on an urgent mission to rescue a friend.

By midnight, despite the wine, or maybe because of it, Tia had regained her perspective. That was the effect Louise had. Louise was essentially a loose cannon who didn't care a damn. That's how she survived.

While rolling up a joint, Louise had spotted Tia's latest book on the side. "You have to be fucking joking!" she'd bawled, pointing at the offending volume. It was *The Meaning of Happiness* by Alan Watts.

"It's actually quite good, Lou. Listen to this: What we are trying to escape from and what we are trying to find are inside ourselves."

She'd seen Louise toying with the idea. Tia had thought she was going to get a clever response, but Louise had stopped herself.

"No wonder you're depressed. As far as Louise Hill is concerned, that entire happiness thing makes life even more complex than it already is. It brings you down. Let's have another joint."

Louise was probably right. She knew she was living a double life which seemed impossible to reconcile. On the one hand, she was Tia the single mum on benefits with two young children. On the other hand, her mind was in a mad kind of wonderland where everything felt achievable and where every new thought which whizzed around her head was brimming with unrealised promise.

One thing she'd kept from Louise was the situation with the landlord's son. If she had let her know the details, she knew exactly what Louise would do. She would turn up with a gang of her mates and give him a good hiding. That wasn't Tia's style. What he'd done was clearly wrong, if not against the law, but challenging him had been too disturbing to consider.

After he had touched her breast, she'd found that £20 of her debt had magically disappeared. It had made her shudder that she'd allowed him to do it. A boundary had been breached; a taboo had been broken. The following week she'd allowed him to touch her again. On that occasion he'd taken his time, rounding her right breast slowly and then, looking at her all the while, he'd helped himself to her left breast. Another £20 had disappeared.

The following week she'd wondered what may happen. Tia and the children had lived on jacket potatoes and beans for five days and Nara had started complaining. Fortunately, he'd been in a hurry; he'd collected the rent as usual and thankfully left without giving her any attention.

Tia had beaten herself up about it; that she'd actually been hoping to be touched up so she could have saved some pennies. There had been nothing in the Alan Watts book or in any other that had addressed this situation or offered her any advice worth having.

After her tits, he'd eventually begun stroking the line of her body and once, albeit briefly, touching her between the thighs. The next month, she'd asked him for £50 for the favour she was offering him.

"Better still, how about £100, in cash?" he'd pulled down his flies. "Imagine it, in a few minutes you will have one hundred smackers in your hand. You could treat the nippers. You could treat yourself."

Her life had become a nightmare. She'd expected a police officer to tap her on the shoulder or, as a punishment, one of her children to fall ill. Her heart was breaking and she'd struggled to read. How could she pretend to be this aspiring thinker when she was cowering in the dirt?

Tia had been fooling no one, least of all herself. Her mother had guessed that something had been amiss, as Tia had kept calling round even when she'd known her father would be at home. But she'd known better than to ask Tia what the matter was. Tia was essentially a private person. Her mother had known to wait until her daughter was ready to talk.

She had been watching the news with the children. In her rasping voice, Teresa May had been describing the obstacles which were in the way before Britain could be free again. An unexpected knock on the door and all the family had looked at one another. It was the landlord's son and behind him a friend. They had been drinking. It had been obvious what they had wanted.

"I can't. The children—"

"Put them in the bedroom."

"No, I won't do that."

"Then, expect an eviction notice on Monday."

"You can't do that."

"Watch me."

Although it would take her over her cash limit, Tia had given the children her phone to watch a YouTube clip on. They'd been sad when the session of play on YouTube had come to an end so quickly, but for Tia it had been the longest fifteen minutes of her life.

CHAPTER 4
March 2018

President Trump expresses praise for the Chinese President Xi being given the role for life.

The Draft Withdrawal Agreement for the UK to leave the European Union is published.

Largely driven by conflict, the number of people going hungry on a regular basis has dramatically increased around the world, reversing decades of progress.

Jon

"Grow your own mythology," Jon said as soon as he got onto his feet. "If you have to believe in anything, believe in yourself. *Gott ist tot.* God is either dead or lies forgotten like an old aunt, alone and fading away in a bedsit in St Mary's. Ask yourself, where do you think all the gods have gone? The sirens and the Minotaur, the Cyclops and the Hydra, where have they gone?"

Nathan Kemp dared to stick his hand up.

"Somewhere in the dark web?" He got the laugh he wanted.

Jon noticed Kemp's quick glance across the hall to Karen Samson. Nothing to worry about; the runt was no competition to him.

"Hilarious, Nathan. At least I know you're awake today. I will tell you where all the gods and the monsters and the ghosts and the beasts have gone. They have gone absolutely nowhere. They started life in our head and there they have remained. The difference now is that we don't externalise them, we don't project them onto the unknown world, because we don't have to. The world is largely known and safe, so instead we internalise them. But they no longer have names, or rather, they are known under different terms. They no longer provide tales in which we can make sense of this complex universe we find ourselves in. What then happens as a consequence?" He loved to pose these rhetorical questions and witness the sea of faces waiting for an answer none of them were brave enough to guess. "Depression. Anxiety. Phobias. Psychosis," he announced, allowing the words an emphasis of silence.

"So mental illness is caused by our lack of mythology?" It was Wilson in the front row.

"Not at all, but there is a connection. I am saying that if we have no way in which to process the vicissitudes of our mysterious minds through religion, myth, allegory, metaphor or story-telling, we will trip up and fall into despair or despondency."

"Mr Fox?" it was none other than Karen. "I'm finding what you are saying truly fascinating, but I am struggling to link it to Critical Theory."

This wasn't the first time a student had questioned his methods. Since his meeting with that snake-in-the-grass Tait, Jon Fox had decided to throw caution to the wind and use his lectures to sound off about his pet subjects. Attendance had been dropping off but why the hell not? He had only two more lectures left before this final module would vanish from the curriculum. Then, if he agreed to the plan, Jon Fox would become the university's dogsbody; an understudy shitting out any crap until a self-styled maestro appeared.

His inclination had been to resign at the sheer effrontery of the matter. He had two or so weeks to make up his mind. He would have preferred sending one of the many caustic letters of resignation he was carrying around in his head, but for the time being decided to hold fire.

"In its essence Karen, I want to get you to think with clarity, integrity and without prejudice. In a real sense, it doesn't really matter what vehicle I use to illustrate any particular concept as it only serves as a means to take you—us—in a certain direction. In an age where every Member of Parliament is a multi-millionaire and child poverty is at a record high, yet all they can do is wave the union jack, we need a new generation to start correcting this trend. And that's all about judgement and decision-making."

He would have clapped if anyone else had beaten him to such an articulate rebuttal. The added effect was that he could see Karen being drawn in. He knew he would have to be careful and more discreet than he had grown accustomed to.

※

The nude photograph he had been sent should have been a turning point to cease. But no, he had chosen it to take it merely as a warning to be more vigilant.

There had been no immediate follow-up call to the photograph, so he had chosen to ignore it. Two weeks later, he'd received another photo. In this one, he'd been as nude as in the first one, but he was laughing straight into the camera. In the corner, he had seen the thigh of the girl who was taking it. A thigh was a thigh but on this one he'd seen part of a tattoo. A fish or a kite? He had racked his brains as to whom it may belong but had come up with nothing.

Another fortnight had whizzed by, and when he had been out with his wife and friends having a meal and drinks with their neighbours, his phone had pinged: *You probably don't remember me. Grace Carver? Ring any bells?*

Not so much as a tinkle let alone a clang. She had gone on to send a series of pictures, variations of the ones before. He had managed to turn the phone over before Lynda had seen the totem of his phallus.

"Someone's popular."

"Bloody Vice Chancellor!" he had rushed to tell her. "We're having a massive reorganisation and the man is freaking out." To emphasise the point, he had rolled his eyes dramatically. Informing his wife about his effective demotion remained a conversation yet to be had.

"That's enough said for today. Read Sylvia Plath's *The Mirror* by next week."

The students automatically rose to their feet, gathering their books and files up as they did so. He overheard someone joke that it was now a poetry appreciation class! Karen made a beeline for him. Unsurprisingly, she had a quick question. The Kemp boy was lingering in the doorway until Jon deftly placed his hand on her arm as he was explaining something to her, a signal to Nathan to disappear. The boy had to give way to the man.

When he'd finally agreed to meet up with Grace Carver, he'd guessed it would be about money. The photos, if made public, would give the university the excuse it needed to sack him. It probably wouldn't do his marriage much good either; let alone the possible effects on the children.

Grace entered the Duke of Wellington where they had arranged to meet without a flicker of recognition on his part.

"How much do you want?" he asked, pulling out his cheque book in one rehearsed movement.

"Not a penny, thank you, Jon." She got herself a gin and tonic. "You don't remember me, do you?"

"Of course, I do."

"It's pretty obvious, Jon. No need to lie."

It turned out that Grace was genuinely uninterested in any money he was more than happy to offer—he had put five grand aside just in case. Her demands though, were much higher: she wanted him to realise what he had done.

She had been a virgin and naively she had taken his invitation to join her in the hotel room as an intention that he wanted her, liked her, even, stupid though it was, loved her. She had fallen for his lies, hook, line and sinker.

As she was speaking, Jon began picking up her little idiosyncrasies; he began recalling some of her mannerisms until eventually it fell into place. That afternoon in the Travelodge. He had put her down as a tubby, chunky student with low self-esteem but the woman now sitting opposite him was none of these things.

"You destroyed me, Jon. I expected you to be in touch after that night, maybe the following day but nothing. Months and months of nothing."

Jon cleared his throat. "What do you want me to do?"

"Say sorry. To be totally and honestly sorry for what you did to me."

"Well, I am sorry as it happens."

"No, nowhere near, I'm afraid. I want you to be sorry to your core for what you did to me and I can imagine, for what you have done and are doing to others."

"Or?" he asked. She refused to answer.

The meeting continued going through his mind when he got home. It was easy to dismiss her as a fantasist, but he realised that he was more of a fantasist than she was. And there were those photographs. He would have to be very careful with Karen.

Lexi

For her fifteenth birthday, her mum and dad took a precarious step and planned an open house. It was true that Lexi was becoming more mobile and when the weather was good, she would sit in the garden. It was equally true that for no reason they could identify, she had days when she struggled to get out of bed and everything appeared to go backward. But all the signs were right. The sky was full of clouds but they were of the light and feathery kind, uninterested in rain and unable to shield a dominant sun.

The family connected with the excitement. Even Harry helped to lay the table in the conservatory. In a show of optimism, they put out chairs under the silver birch which stood in the middle of the lawn. The sea beyond the garden was a brilliant azure blue, which they took as a desire to be part of the celebration.

She had already received a few gifts but by far the most valued was the book of *Modern Women Poets* sent by her great Aunt, Ursula Bird. Lexi thought this was particularly generous as, despite living less than thirty miles away, she had only met her handful of times.

"She's a writer," her dad explained. "She's been writing stuff since she was your age. With not so much as a poem published, a few years ago she decided to self-publish. She's got quite a collection now."

Lexi asked him to get her to send her one.

"You do it," her dad said. "I'm sure she would love to hear from you."

Her mum's sister was the first to arrive with her three children. Other relatives drifted in, unburdening themselves of gifts, but Lexi didn't come alive until her three mates turned up together. They went through the traditions of the occasion — the usual toast from her dad, the opening of presents and the blowing out of candles. Later the adults locked themselves in a slightly inebriated discussion about the EU Withdrawal Bill, which her dad thought he had won when he slammed his fist on the table declaring it was nothing less than an obscene power grab by ministers.

The younger children were running round in circles in a game of changing rules. This gave Lexi and her mates the opportunity to disappear onto a bench located in a small recess in the side garden.

Lexi told them about a visit she'd had from Jacob the previous day. He had bought her a gift of perfume, Eternity. Wow! Not cheap! As usual, he had been lost for words but suddenly without warning, he'd tried to kiss her, placing his hand on her right tit at the same time. The kiss had misfired and he had caught her on the corner of the mouth. Shocked at his own bravery, Jacob had retracted his hand as quickly as he had put it there. This story sent them into hysterics.

"And what did you do?"

"I waited a minute, then brought him back round to me, placed his hand on my boob and kissed him."

"You slut!" said Carla. "What happened next?"

"He went as red as a beetroot, mumbled a happy birthday and left."

Typically, the three of them, Molly, Carla and Lexi, relied on Rayn to keep the conversation flowing but it was obvious Rayn was not herself. She was much quieter than usual. Rayn didn't do quiet. When they risked sharing a cigarette, Lexi asked her what was going on.

"Honestly, nothing."

"That's total BS, Rayn. What's going on?"

It turned out that Freya and her clan had taken note of part of Lexi's threat whilst ignoring the sentiment. She'd never contacted Lexi again, as instructed, and taking it one step further, had retaliated by unfriending her on Facebook. Freya hadn't stopped bothering Rayn though. Rayn had kept most of it to herself but recently they had upped their assault on her. On various social platforms Rayn had been depicted as a weirdo, a lesbo, a wackjob or all three. The previous week, a photograph of her had been pinned to the main school notice board. Horns had been drawn growing out of her head, her teeth were blacked in and underneath were the words: *Please keep away from this nutter — it's catching!*

Carla was all for going to her house or telling her parents or the school or the police. Bullying is against the law, you know. But Rayn, having realised she had spilt the beans about her dilemma, tried to backtrack and play down the impact. When she insisted they drop the subject and get back to something more interesting, like Jacob's sex drive, or lack of, they acquiesced and went on to other things. When it came to leaving, they all hugged, as usual. Lexi noticed though that Rayn was holding her a second too long. Facing her, she knew Rayn was struggling but when asked again, she shrugged and went her way.

The party exhausted Lexi and she was back in her bedroom by eight. After she'd texted Rayn to make sure she was alright, she opened up the book of poetry her aunt had sent her. Up to this point, Lexi hadn't taken poetry that seriously. It was merely one theme amongst all the other subjects she was studying at home either with books, via the Internet or on YouTube. The power of the words fascinated her. One sentence could transport her into an entirely different world. A few lines and she could be in a desert, in love, flying through the air, burning in hell. It intrigued her that a certain formulation of words could speak directly to her, provide meaning, describe beauty.

Her favourite at the moment was Sylvia Plath's *The Mirror*. Lexi wondered how Plath could have written such a mesmerising poem about something as mundane as a mirror. But she had, comparing it to a god, an impartial and indifferent god, indifferent to its fate and purpose, merely swallowing what presents itself, the absence of time contrasting with the repetition of days. Plath introduced a woman exploring her true nature in the mirror—leaning in too much may cause her to fall and drown.

Putting the book down, she realised she hadn't heard back from Rayn.

She texted again — *what are you up to? Nothing dodgy, I hope! X*

She read a few more poems and fell asleep, her lamp still on. About an hour later, she suddenly came to. She immediately picked up her phone. Nothing from Rayn. This was unlike Rayn, the queen of texting. She phoned her and it went directly to messages. This was not right. She called both Molly and Carla and asked if they had heard anything. Neither had. Lexi started shouting for her mum.

"What on earth is the matter? You're waking up the little ones."

"It's Rayn, Mum. Something's wrong — she's not replied to my messages, she's not answering her phone."

"Lexi, not everyone is like you, you know. Maybe she's sleeping like you should be."

"You're really not listening, Mum." At that, Lexi phoned Rayn's parents.

"Go up to Rayn, NOW!"

The phone thrown to one side; Lexi could hear the drama unfold. She could hear Rayn's mother screaming. She could hear people running up and down stairs, the calling of an ambulance. Listening, Lexi cried, her mum holding her.

She found out the details the following day. They had found Rayn hanging from her wardrobe, her school tie around her neck. She was already blue and not breathing but her father had pulled her to the floor and thumped her chest, shouting for his wife to call an ambulance. By the time it had arrived, Rayn was unconscious but breathing. A minute later and they would have lost her.

Dexter

It was a perfect day for fishing. The water was calm, almost without a ripple, reflecting the heavy bank of clouds caught on the horizon. Every sound arose without echo or reverberation, captured and strangely muffled.

Dexter had organised his boys, Andrew and Danny, to be ready to leave as early as possible. By some miracle they'd made it to the end of the stone pier by eight in the morning.

Despite the signs banning feathering, Dexter was after mackerel. It was early in the year for shoals to come this close to shore and though stocks had been dwindling in the last ten years, he had already been out and caught a dozen. He had shown the boys a million times how to fish for mackerel.

Each line held six feathers hiding six hooks. The first job was to uncork each hook. Casting out was something of a knack and it took the boys some time to master it. The trick was to let the catch off the reel and whip it swiftly overhead. Done properly the line should take off and hooks and weights plop into the water about twenty metres away.

Much to Andrew's annoyance, Danny, the younger brother, managed to perfect the technique first. He was also the first to land a mackerel. It was too small to keep so Dexter unhooked it and threw it back into the sea, telling it to go and bring back its mum and dad.

Their bucket still empty, they decided to eat lunch early. Out came the flask of coffee, the salad sandwiches, the pork pies and the crisps.

"So, what's a-happening lads? How's school going?"

Andrew was studying the solar system and the moon landings.

"Hard to believe, Dad, that those rockets got up there," he said, pointing to the moon which was rising pale and translucent over St Aldhelm's Head.

Dexter was already shaking his head. "I'm going to have to have a word with your teacher. It's been long known that the moon landings were one ginormous pile of lies."

"Not so, Dad. They even bought moon rocks back."

"Don't you 'not so' me. All of it was a hoax and took place in Pinewood studios or some such place. It was all staged so the Americans could get one over on the Russians."

In a bid to prevent an argument, Danny put his hand on his brother's arm, but Andrew was eleven and not a kid anymore, and he resented this put-down by his dad.

"Of course, it happened. It's recorded in books, it's on the internet."

Dexter laughed at his son's naivety. "You need to think for yourself, Andrew, not listen to others, especially teachers."

"Then why do you send us to school?"

"Good point. I wonder why myself."

Andrew didn't quite know what to do. He was learning, he was enjoying his studies and here was his own father trashing it. He wanted to yell at him or punch him but in the end, he told him that he was talking rubbish.

It was Dexter's turn to become riled. "Okay, Mr Know-all. If you want me to spell it out, the reasons are," his voice was raised, he counted out his points one by one on his fingers. "One, the American flag was fluttering, when there's no wind on the moon. Two, the shadows don't match up. Three, in all the photos of so-called space, you never see one star. Four, in places you can see the rocks have been set down evenly, some are even marked with letters. Should I go on?"

"Please don't, Dad," Danny piped up.

"Fair enough," he agreed, calming down.

"All I am asking you boys to do is think for yourself. Don't just digest wholesale everything the teachers tell you. Even gravity is just a theory."

The mackerel started biting about an hour later, the simmering shoals evident under the smooth shallows. They called it upside rain. They started reeling them in but since their lunchtime discussion, they were pretty much fishing in silence. Much to the delight of dozens of seagulls coming out from nowhere, Dexter beheaded and gutted the fish as they were caught. They ended up with twenty-two, with Danny getting half of them. Beginner's luck, his dad told him.

As soon as they got home, the boys disappeared to their bedrooms, leaving Dexter to return the fishing gear to the shed. He bagged sixteen mackerel for the freezer and laid out six, ready to be cooked for their dinner.

That evening after a meal of sweet mackerel, scalloped chips and peas, he was sitting beer in hand watching a programme about UFOs when Dee marched into the lounge and switched off the television.

"I'll have you know I was enjoying that." To his surprise, her brother, Chris followed her in. Dexter had always considered Chris to be a smug git.

"Chris, my man, what brings you here?"

Dee and Chris sat down on the sofa. Dee had a large glass of Sauvignon Blanc.

"What's going on here? I feel like I'm on trial." He tried to laugh but nobody was laughing.

"It's your turn to listen, Dexter. I bought Chris over to make sure you hear what I am saying and take some notice."

"I'm not sure what this is about but I won't have it." Dexter went to get up but this evoked a similar response in Chris. He sat back down and took a swig of beer. "Alright, out with it. I want to get back to my programme."

"I want you to stop."

"Stop what exactly."

"You know. All this conspiracy stuff. I'm sick of it, absolutely sick of it. Always on that fucking laptop, morning and night. Walking around like a zombie waiting to spill some piece of crap as soon as the telly's on or someone says something about the world. I've put up with this shit for months and months. But turning on the boys, Dexter. That's where I draw the line. The boys told me everything you said to them today. Really, Dexter? Shoving that baloney about the moon landings down their throats. And gravity's a theory is it?" She gulped back her wine and looking directly at him, allowed the glass to slip from her hand. It shattered into a million pieces. "Pretty good theory, I would say."

"Dee, you've been a misbeliever since day one. You need to open up to the truth, not close me down to it. How many times have I told you they're not conspiracy theories? The true conspiracy is hiding the truth from us. Even the president of the United States knows this much."

Dee looked at her brother in disbelief.

"You need to listen to what Dee's saying, Dexter."

"And you need to go fuck yourself."

"Let me put it plainly, Dexter," Dee continued. "If I hear any more, even the slightest reference to any conspiracy theory whatsoever, I'm leaving you and I'm taking the boys."

"What? You can't do that," he pleaded but already the fight was draining from his voice.

"Watch me."

Ursula

In the last week Ursula had received two favourable reviews of her book, *The Mindless Clock*. One was unfortunately delivered in person.

Greg Andrews turned up on her doorstep at the ridiculous time of ten in the morning. She had barely finished the mammoth task of harnessing up the dogs for her virtual ski ride to the park when he knocked on the door. The dogs went mad. Even Desmond managed a singular bark of outrage. Confusing them further she put them back into the kitchen and shut them in. Opening the door, she had to bite her tongue to stop herself from swearing. Greg stood there with his innate grin, holding her book.

"All I can say is wow! It's a classic, Ursula. Witty, clever, perfectly rounded. Characters were totally believable. I loved, loved, loved Mrs E. Piper. Very Mrs Havisham."

"Always good to get feedback. Could you post a review on Amazon?"

"Consider it done!"

"Sorry, I can't keep you; the dogs need walking."

"Not a problem. I could walk with you. We could talk about the book."

"Good idea but Carlo hates strangers and would cause such a fuss."

"Fair enough, Ursula. Just wanted to say — it was an excellent read."

The second review came via email from the old guy, Matthew Price, who she had met at last year's Book Fayre: *Progressing onto the rest of your collection. If I know where to find them?* She thanked him for his appreciation and told him how to get hold of the sequel, *The Purple Taboo*.

Ever since she'd had her light bulb moment about embarking on a new novel, Ursula hadn't written a single sentence. She had penned some reviews, edited a novella for a friend and had written a piece for the local newspaper on creative writing. As for a novel, not a word. She reassured herself that it had never gone away and was always aware of its presence, or better put, of its absence. She knew she was going to write it. What she didn't know at this point was whether that day would be the day she would begin.

She walked the dogs, taking them for a particularly long sketch along the sands. This was more hassle than it was worth; Ahmed wanted the ball thrown continuously, Desmond wouldn't let go of his toy and Carlos wanted to say hello to every mutt he came across. The dogs were having the time of their life, so she felt duty bound to put on a brave face and walk from one pier to the other.

She was just passing the jubilee clock when someone called out her name.

"I cannot believe it, Ursula Prudence Bird, or should I say Greening?"

Ursula hadn't heard her middle name spoken out loud for years and had hoped never to hear it again. What's more, she had reverted back to Bird on the day of Robert's funeral.

Doubly irritated, she knew instantly who this was—Moira Waters—but when she turned to face her, she hardly recognised her. Always a little woman, Moira was now as small as a child. Age had patterned her face into a map of A and B roads and somehow she had lost her two front teeth.

Ursula's preferred bubble of anonymity had been burst. She had no choice but to go along with it. She and Moira had gone to Grammar School together. Never close, she bumped into her every few years.

"I heard about Robert. Such sad news. It must have knocked you for six?"

"You could say that."

"I remember your wedding day. You looked like a couple made in heaven." Ursula had forgotten that Moira had turned up at the church. "You know, Vera and I both envied you. To think of meeting someone in your middle age. And such a kind and handsome chap. We thought you were the luckiest person."

Happily, at that moment, Ahmed got into a barking match with another Jack Russell. Ursula made her excuses and hurried off, leaving Moira standing there, mid-sentence.

By the time she arrived back home, the words kind and handsome had gnawed a hole through her skull. The words cruel and grotesque would have been much more suitable adjectives when applied to that complete shithead.

An outward indicator of her anger, she uncorked the Amontillado Sherry and poured herself a large tumbler full. If only that woman had known the truth.

Seven years ago, almost to the day, Robert had demonstrated how kind and handsome he really was. After the book fayre episode, there had followed a couple of months of relative calm.

Whether he was ashamed or had exhausted himself for the time being or was finding sport elsewhere, she hadn't known or cared and certainly hadn't dared ask. Once she had dropped the box of her soiled books in the bin, she'd vowed never to refer to the incident again. She'd known that it wouldn't be the end of his terror and she had also known that it would only be a matter of time before it resumed—when rather than if.

It had come out later that he had won two-hundred on the horses and had disappeared into the Swan to celebrate his winnings. He'd bought drinks for his cronies and any other chancer who'd shown an interest. Two hundred was soon twenty. High on cider, he'd stumbled back into the bookies, confident that this was his lucky day. Taking it for granted that his winning streak would continue, he'd randomly placed bets on horses he had never heard of. Every time, he'd lost. By four in the afternoon, he was four-hundred and fifty pounds down. Becoming increasingly aggressive, the manager had had to ask Mr 'kind and handsome' to leave.

As soon as he'd come home, he'd laid into Ursula, amongst other things calling her a slut, a whore and an ugly dunce. She'd stomached them all but the insult on her intellect by this empty-brained moron was too much. At the height of their shouting, Rossetti had been going mad, barking insistently and tugging at his trouser leg. When Robert had pushed Ursula back onto the sofa, the dog had continued her defence until Robert had scooped her up in one hand and thrown her as hard as he could against the wall. Ursula could still hear the agonising yelp even now.

"If I hear one word from you, you're next!" he'd said before leaving the house.

She'd buried Rossetti in the garden. She'd wept another prayer while Desmond had silently looked on. Afterwards she'd calmly moved all her stuff into the spare bedroom. Neither had mentioned the move. Every now and then, Robert would come in drunk and rape her but she'd decided not to speak, not to resist, hoping this horror would eventually stop. She'd known she could endure his lust—as long as he'd returned to his bed and left her alone.

She turned on the news and listened to the testimony of a Rohingya woman who had lost her home, been evicted from the village she was born in and was unaware of where her eldest son was. This was a woman who was suffering an evil brought on because of her culture and through no fault of her own. This was courage. If this woman had courage, why not her? Why not Ursula Prudence Bird?

That evening in bed, the dogs laid out in their preferred positions, she took out her grey notepad and wrote the first two sentences.

It is said that it is harder to heal than to kill. What if, my friend, it is necessary to kill before any healing is possible?

Matthew

It was Matthew's first day as a volunteer in the local food bank. He had been filling his time reading novels at the fastest rate in his life, and pottering around the garden but had reached the point where these self-indulgent activities had cried out for a balance to do something for others. Initially, he had been plagued with misgivings, wondering if this was another manifestation of his old faith. He'd concluded that it wasn't, it was a humanitarian gesture. Introducing God into the equation simply interfered with the basic relationship of one human to another.

He'd thought about working in charity shops but that was essentially about selling crap nobody else wanted. He'd thought of the Samaritans, concluding that he was too close to and fatalistic about his own death to be of any real use.

His next-door neighbour, Sandra Unwin, had suggested helping out at the food bank. He'd liked the idea and had gone online as soon as he was indoors again. He had been shocked and outraged to find that there were hundreds of food banks up and down the country and that some families were totally dependent on them. The descriptions of the plight of some people echoed in his head the memory of 1952.

He held memories of going to bed starving after the one meal of the day and shivering in the terrible winter. But that was then and this was now. Britain was one of the largest economies in the world. What had happened? His offer as a volunteer was readily accepted, although it grated on him because it was his status as a former member of the clergy that had eased him in.

Sandra was kind enough to drop him at the town bridge. He looked forward to the short walk along the harbour. He had forgotten however that he would have to pass one church he had only unhappy recollections of. His experiences there had certainly done their bit to further undermine his faith.

He'd been acting as a locum priest and had been assigned to this parish while he'd waited for the post to be filled. Ostensibly, it had seemed a pleasant enough church with a healthy congregation and a full choir. A few weeks in and he'd genuinely felt he was making a difference.

The woman who'd arranged the flowers, a Mrs Lawson, had said that they weren't used to the type of sermons he'd preached. "In a good way, you understand," she'd added. "But we notice you don't mention God much."

"Implicit in everything I say," he'd told her.

Matthew had arrived early one Sunday. He hadn't done his sermon as yet, so had thought he would walk the beach in search of inspiration. He'd ended up walking to the end of the stone pier and watched a father and his two young boys fishing for mackerel. Just the symbolism he'd needed. Still only half eight, he'd had plenty of time to get his thoughts down on paper.

He had assumed the church would be empty but he'd found the vestry door unlocked. He'd walked straight in to find his deacon, the choir master and one of the choir boys. Their rapid movements and their smiling greetings had made him suspicious. He'd asked them why they were there so early. The choir master, Sid Brigs, had rushed towards him with a sheet of music.

"We're trying to work out the best way to tackle the soprano section of this morning's anthem. As you know, Darren here is doing our solo."

He had tried to take no notice. He actually hadn't seen anything untoward and had tried to blame his warped imagination. It had probably been nothing but something about their hasty movements coupled with an underlying feeling of nervousness had played on his mind.

He'd begun watching them, observing how and when they had spoken to the boys. And he had sensed they were likewise looking at him. Eventually, he'd pulled Darren aside and asked him if everything was alright. He'd shrugged but as he'd left, muttered that he could do without all the medical checks.

The following week, Matthew called them into his office and asked them what was going on, why had Darren been talking about medical checks? Brigs had said that the boys did get confused.

"Well, I have heard enough to write to the bishop."

The deacon had actually sworn at him. "You waltz in here, imagining all sorts of fucking things."

The response had come back by return of post. The bishop had failed to address any of his concerns but instead had informed him that he had found a permanent replacement for his current position: *Therefore, with immediate effect, your services are no longer required in Weymouth but I have the perfect slot for you in the North of the County.*

꩜

Matthew was allowed in the back entrance to the food bank. He was warmly welcomed and the organiser, Pat Myers introduced him to all the other assistants.

"This really has become an industry since the Conservatives took office."

He loved it. The three hours were over in a flicker. What amazed him was the courtesy of the staff towards their 'customers'. They exhibited an authentic patience he had hardly ever witnessed in church. Without judgement, people were helped to select what they required. If, for example, they learnt that they had two or three children, they would recommend this or that product, tucking it into their carrier bags before they could object.

Two women customers stood out to Matthew. Gum-chewing Louise asked him if he had any vodka in the back. When he informed her it was unlikely, she said it was a pity.

"You would definitely get more customers."

"I think we may have enough already."

She would swap all this food for a bottle any day. Her friend, Tia, a young woman in her early twenties was quieter but clearly enjoyed her friend's sense of humour. Matthew spotted a copy of Jung's memoirs in her handbag.

"Ah, have I found a fellow fan of Carl Jung?"

"I'm afraid so."

"In any other age," he said before he could think, "he would have been a priest or a shaman."

"I completely agree," she said, smiling.

"Well," said Louise, "personally, I'd rather read the phone directory."

Tia

Though she had no desire to get dressed, Tia understood she had to go through the motions. Katherine, her neighbour, picked Nara up on the way to school with her friends. She made a huge effort to be normal but everything inside of her felt exactly the opposite. Her mother would be harder to convince. She arrived after nine to pick up Kojo, who squeaked in excitement at her.

"You alright, Tia?"

"One hundred percent!" she said, too passionately.

Her mother looked at her sidelong. "If you needed anything, you would say, wouldn't you?"

"You know me, Mum," again too breezy.

"Yes, I do know you. I am your mother."

When her mother left with Kojo, Tia stood at the gate to the flats, waving frantically. As soon as they disappeared, she rushed back into the flat, tore off her clothes and crawled into bed. She couldn't hate herself more than she did at that moment. It didn't help that the memory of the other night kept thrusting itself into her thoughts.

She and Louise had persuaded Katherine to have the children for an evening while they went out to let off steam. Tia hadn't told a soul about the landlord's son but every time she thought about him, it was another step towards madness. The dam was near to bursting.

The night before, Louise had been taken aback by how fast Tia was drinking—an observation which was quite something for Louise. They'd gone into one club, necked some more cocktails and just to wind up the ogling men, they'd started dancing flirtatiously with each other. Inevitably they began chatting to a particular group of men. Louise was snogging one of them within five minutes. She really didn't care a damn. But Tia was too drunk; she'd broken away from them and barged past the bouncer to get outside. An hour or two later she'd woken up in a shop doorway. A policeman had been looking down on her. She'd thought he was there to help her, but he'd calmly unzipped his flies and pissed on her.

Today she just wanted to stay in bed and die. It wasn't until lunchtime that she managed to break the grip of her trance and swing her legs to the side of the bed and sit up. She had to get to the food bank soon, as it closed in an hour.

But no sooner had she thought this, she broke into a fit of anger. With one sweep of her arm, everything on her make-shift dressing table went crashing to the ground. She ripped madly at her clothes, smashed a glass against the wall, pulled at the curtains until they were left tangling like a defeated flag.

Finally she attacked her books, the books she loved, the books which opened up new worlds to her, the books which would take her away from all this chaos.

"Who the fuck are you trying to kid, you fucking slut?" With that, she tore Jung's memoirs in half: it felt more like she was tearing her own heart in half.

When her anger abated, she was standing in the middle of the mess she had created, looking bewildered and confused. Numbly she walked into the shower room and turned on the cold setting. Still in her underwear she got in and sat down, almost oblivious to the freezing water. Afterwards she blindly dressed, put on her coat and left for the food bank.

The kindness of the helpers was suffocating, almost cruel, but picking up her cans of beans and her loaf of bread and a tube of spaghetti, she told herself to just get through it. One volunteer, an old man called Matthew, who she had been talking to over the last few weeks, tried to pass the time with her but Tia kept her head down and said nothing.

Relieved to get out, Tia sat on one of the benches which looked out to sea and rolled a cigarette.

"May I join you?" It was Matthew. She didn't answer him but he sat down anyway. "May I have one? A roll-up?"

Absent-mindedly, she gave him the tobacco and papers. He fiddled around with the papers until reluctantly she took them back and rolled him one.

"Haven't had a roll-up since ... let me see, 1971, I think."

They sat smoking in silence.

"They say you're a vicar."

"Oh, do they? Not anymore. I said goodbye to all that over a year ago."

"You don't believe in God anymore?"

"Not God and certainly not the church."

"Would you hear my confession?"

"I didn't know you were religious?"

"I'm not."

"Sorry, even when I was a vicar, I didn't do confessions. But I'm quite happy to listen."

When she started, she couldn't stop. She told him everything, didn't spare him any of the details: her abuse by a teacher, her failed relationships, her unloving father, the landlord's son and finally the policemen pissing on her in a shop doorway.

"I think I need another cigarette, Tia." She duly rolled him and herself another.

"Doesn't it make my dream to become a nurse seem absolutely pathetic?"

It was after his first drag that he answered her.

"Not at all. Tia, let's get you out of there." Tia was about to challenge him when he put out his hand. "Just listen. I am going to loan you—loan, I say, it's not a gift—enough money to get you out of that awful place and get you and the children into somewhere better, somewhere you deserve to be."

"I can't do that."

"Yes, you can and yes, you will. I have the money just sitting in my bank account doing sod all. At least, a loan would make good use of it."

"Thank you, Matthew but I couldn't do that."

"What are you doing now?"

He persuaded her to go with him into a letting agency. Matthew told them what was required: a house, not a flat, three bedrooms, preferably on the south side of the town bridge. A vacant semi-furnished property had just become available.

"Super," Matthew said. "Tia, take a seat down there and look at the details and see what you think."

She duly read the details, folded the paper and joined them at the desk.

"It's perfect but it's not going to happen."

"It already has. It's all paid up, the deposit with twelve months rent. If you don't move now, it will be empty for a year which seems a dreadful shame."

Four hours later, Tia was pushing an overloaded pushchair over the town bridge — Kojo was in there somewhere, Galway the goldfish was swinging from side to side in a plastic bag of water. Both mother and daughter had bloated rucksacks on their backs. With a free hand, Tia was dragging a black bag of clothes behind her. She'd decided to leave behind everything they couldn't carry. In the end, things were unimportant. But she had Jung's memoirs with her, newly sellotaped and wedged under Kojo's pushchair. On the town bridge, she stopped, suddenly thinking about the implications of what she was doing. Could Matthew be trusted? Was he another predator in a new guise?

"Everything alright, Mum?" Nara asked her.

"Yes," she said, brushing Nara's hair back from her face. "Everything is alright." And the procession to her new place began once more.

She said nothing to her landlord and gave no forwarding address. She never went back to the flat again and neither did she set foot in that street.

CHAPTER 5
October 2018

Greta Thunberg continues to sit outside the Swedish Parliament on her solo 'School Strike for the Climate'.

670,000 people join a protest in London against Brexit.

Theresa May appeals to 'patriots' to stop Johnson's leadership bid.

Jon

It was Lynda's idea to go out for a meal. She said it was the anniversary of their first date twenty-two years ago. Jon wasn't aware of whether it was or not, but as it was unusual for them to dine out together, he was more than happy to agree. When she told him it would be her treat though, Jon became apprehensive.

She chose Alexandra's Restaurant; the original restaurant they had dined in was now a charity shop. Jon wouldn't have known the difference anyway.

The new term had started and he was no longer listed on the permanent team of staff. He had seen his course vanish without ceremony. The last two lectures he'd thoroughly enjoyed. He'd demonstrated how good poetry could be used to hone critical skills and drill down to the essence of meaning.

Having got wind of his sinking favour, the last one had been attended by about half of the students who'd applied for the module but Jon was past caring and had used it as a bombast against the elite. He'd blamed William the Conqueror for not only invading a country that had nothing to do with him but for getting rid of the Anglo-Saxon hierarchy in the south and the Danish hierarchy in the north and substituting almost all of them with his own Norman cronies. Ever since this, the elite of the royals and the rich had secured the positions of power and influence forever. Ask yourself how many members of parliament are wealthy and privileged. Ask yourselves how many of them went to Eton. The remaining students had enjoyed this opinionated diatribe, aware that they were witnessing a ranting man who had nothing to lose.

He'd had no intention of returning as a lackey fill-in — a sort of academic putty for the university — but he'd kept his cards close to his chest. Technically, he was still on the payroll. He was paid for the summer and in a brilliant stroke of mastery, in his opinion, he had put in a request for a two-month sabbatical. This had ostensibly been to finish a paper he had started years before on the impact of critical thinking on future employment. He'd put forward the case that he wished to complete this university-commissioned project before beginning his new role. Naturally, he'd had no intention of finishing the paper or, for that matter, taking up his new 'fabricated' post, but they couldn't find any good reason to refuse him. It was already October and he was still on full pay.

There had also been a dearth of female interest in his life. Karen, his previous target, had backfired and he'd suspected Grace Carver was behind it. At first, all had been going swimmingly with Karen. She had responded to all his cues and was demonstrating a growing interest in him, when suddenly, without explanation, she had dropped him and left his course. The conference he had planned for her down in Exeter University had been cancelled, along with the overnighter in the Hotel Du Vin.

He'd ended up chatting up one of the university admin staff, Clare Flowers. He'd thought he was doing her a favour but afterwards it had become clear that she'd been thinking about it the other way round. After two encounters, it had fizzled out into nothing and he'd spent an inordinate amount of time fathoming out how to exit the university without going anywhere near the reception office she was based in.

Grace was still in touch with him. Despite him trying to pay her off and have done with it, she was still hanging out for 'genuine' contrition for his actions. The few times they had met she had dismissed his apologies as a contrivance to either get rid of her or, more probably, to stop her from uploading the photographs onto Facebook, or whichever social platform she favoured. When he'd met Grace, he'd been perversely hoping to say sorry via the medium of lovemaking and had cursed his memory for not providing more details of the beauty who had sat opposite him.

As he was getting ready for the anniversary dinner, it both surprised and amused him that he may well get lucky with his wife. The last time they had actually made out together was when they both drank too much on New Year's Eve, ten months ago.

When Lynda emerged from her bedroom, he would have bet on it; she was wearing a slimming black dress and a simple gold necklace with matching earrings. She knew he loved this outfit: he received the message she was sending his way.

The taxi arrived smack on seven and they drew up to Alexandra's before their booking was due. This gave them the perfect excuse to nip into the pub next door for a quick drink.

"A toast," said Lynda, "Twenty-two years tonight. Would you ever have believed it?"

"Not at all. I thought it was going to be a one-night stand and then only if I played my cards right."

"Thank you very much." They chinked glasses.

"All things considered, I think we have done well. Long may it continue."

They clinked glasses again but Jon became aware that she hadn't echoed his sentiment.

The reason for this celebration became clearer when they were at their table in the restaurant, sipping the house red and waiting for their food to arrive.

"Thank you for agreeing to this, Jon. I thought it would give us a chance to discuss some changes I have in mind."

"You're sounding very official, Lynda. You're not at work now."

"There's no easy way to say this, Jon. I've met someone."

"Nothing unusual there then."

"No. I've met someone."

"And?"

"And we're in love. I want a divorce, Jon, I want you out of the house, Jon."

"Will you stop Jonning me, for fuck's sake."

"I think we both knew this would come along some day."

"No, no, no, I didn't expect this to come along some day. I expected everything to tick over as it always has done, you doing your thing, me doing mine."

"Well, that's not going to happen."

"It is in my books."

"Your books are full of lies, Jon. I'm asking for a divorce. Simple and straightforward. And I'm happy to give you until Christmas to get out."

"Sounds like you have worked it all out but you may have forgotten a little something. Sophie and Victoria for example."

"They're both on board."

"What? You spoke with the girls before you spoke to me?"

"Reflecting the order of importance. They have seen it coming for a while. Anyway, Victoria will be at Uni so she's fine. Sophie hardly sees you anyway."

"Bitch."

"Oh, come on, Jon. You've got a decent job. You'll be able to buy a place of your own. You're going to have the freedom you have always craved."

Lexi

Day one: the blog goes live. Rayn and Lexi watched the screen for a whole hour before they got a like. It was only Molly but they both shrieked with delight. Carla followed ten minutes later and left a comment: *Never let a stumble in the road be the end of your journey.*

Obviously she got that straight from the internet but that didn't take anything away from the sentiment. Rayn replied in their chat room that a stumble may even be the beginning of a new journey. Carla came back straight away with a smiling emoji, followed by a thumbs-up.

"There we go," Rayn announced, "our very first conversation on our very first blog!"

It had been two hundred and nineteen days since Lexi had shouted down the phone at Rayn's parents. It had been a living hell. Lexi had arrived at Rayn's house with her mum first thing that morning. Except for Rayn's mum, who was at the hospital, the family were still up, drinking tea and trying to make sense of the situation. Rayn's siblings had been told that their sister had been suddenly taken ill.

"Like what happened to Lexi?" asked her brother.

Time had frozen in the days immediately afterwards. Lexi had been in a sort of fog; a fog in which she couldn't read or write or watch television or listen to music. Sia had had nothing to say to her.

Lexi had kept quizzing her mum about it until, exasperated that she'd had no useful insights to give her daughter, she'd told her to stop dwelling on it. But Lexi had wanted to do the very opposite. She had wanted to understand what was going on. Her bestie had tried to end her life, finish it completely, to disappear.

Rayn had become so overwhelmed that her thoughts had become enemies and her feelings had attacked her like a virus. At the moment when she had put the tie around her neck, at that moment everything—family, friends, school, memory—everything in her past and present life had amounted to nothing compared with the insufferable longing to end it all.

Lexi had wanted to know what had led to this desperate moment. The only thing she had been able to manage was to dip in and out of poetry, allowing a phrase to float in her mind, unattached, lost and without meaning.

Rayn's mum and dad had phoned the night of the incident to tell them that Rayn was going to be alright, that they had taken her out of intensive care and had moved her onto an open ward. The staff had asked for no visitors until Rayn had significantly improved.

Three days later, Rayn's parents had come to the house. As soon as Mrs Notley had entered the lounge, she'd burst into tears, fallen to the floor and hugged Lexi's knees. Between sobs, she had praised Lexi for saving her daughter, for saving Rayn. It had all been very dramatic, to the point of being disturbing. Lexi's mum had joined in with tears of her own, leaving the two men standing there unsure how to express themselves. It had been a relief when they'd left. Lexi had promised to visit Rayn the following day.

Lexi had refused to use her wheelchair or her stick and had insisted on putting on a smart outfit. She'd refused to take flowers or chocolates or grapes—she'd known Rayn would have plenty of them—instead, she'd taken her own copy of the *Poetry of Presence* anthology. She'd written on the front page, quoting from one of the poems: *It hurts to love wide open.*

The parents, going downstairs to the cafe, had at least had the sense to leave them alone together.

"Well, look where I am."

Lexi had pulled the covers back and got in beside her. "Look where we both are."

Rayn had been discharged the following day. Lexi had assumed she would want to be left alone but that was definitely not the case.

The day after that, Rayn had turned up unannounced with hidden fags and gin as if nothing had happened. Despite being aware of the shadow they were avoiding, they'd been quick to get back to what was familiar to them. Once the gin hit, Lexi couldn't hold back any longer. She'd asked her about what had happened that night.

Naturally, there had been tears but Lexi hadn't let up. She'd wanted to know the ins and outs of her friend's experience.

"You really are a heartless cow!" Rayn had complained.

"Just a curious one. Now spare me nothing, tell me everything. I want to know how a wonderful human being like you can even consider topping herself."

It had already been getting dark by the time Rayn told Lexi how she'd found herself waking up in hospital.

"It took me a few minutes to put two and two together. Mum and Dad were all over me of course, but my head felt like a lead weight. It was only when my eyes fell on a carrier bag of my clothing that I realised what I had done. The tip of the tie was just showing. My dad saw that I had seen it and rushed over and put it under the bed. But for some reason, I was thinking of bees. The black and yellow of the tie made me think of bees and how our teacher had told us that bees never want to sting you because if they do, they die."

Although only months ago, it all seemed like ancient history now. The school had held an inquiry and revisited their bullying policy but Rayn hadn't said who the main bullies were. Enough was enough and she'd known there would be no comeback. She'd been right; it was almost as if the bullies who had delighted in hurting her were, for no obvious reason, afraid of her now and avoided her at all costs.

The blog had been Lexi's idea but had Rayn loved it. They'd called it the Buzzline—for all those struggling to fly, bullies and victims alike.

They knew it was a daft title with the head teacher advising them that the title may not attract the people they were hoping to. Rayn wrote her own story down. Lexi added some of her poetry. One poem caught the comic twist to the frankness they were aspiring to: *It never Rayns but it pours*.

They checked the site after dinner: over five hundred likes and a couple of stories of abuse and triumph.

Not bad at all.

Dexter

Kirsty—known locally as Thirsty Kirsty because of her love of real ale—had set Dexter a challenge. She wanted a tattoo which was original and unique to her. She didn't mind paying for it. She didn't care how long it took as long as it was exclusive to her and there wasn't a soul in the world with the same image. Dexter was more than happy to take up the dare.

"Come on, you have to give me some idea what you want. A tattoo is for life you know, not just Christmas."

Kirsty conceded the point and threw him a few ideas. She liked whales. She liked stars. Oh yes, and she liked old sailing ships.

"Very helpful," he said, rolling his eyes. "Come back in a week and I'm sure I'll have something for you." He bought a cheap A2 pad and started doodling.

Since Dee had given him an ultimatum, Dexter had behaved himself. He'd stopped bothering people with his theories and never mentioned another word to his boys. Any 'studying' was confined to his work laptop during quiet times. He'd continued to unravel mysteries about the world but he'd worked hard at keeping his learning to himself. If he came across a fellow believer, then — and only then — had he allowed himself free rein to explore new ideas or exchange old ones. He didn't want to admit it but life was actually easier not having to explain what was happening around the globe. His mates had begun re-engaging with him. More importantly than this, his family were definitely happier in their ignorance.

His work always afforded him the prospect of engrossing himself fully into the job at hand. Kirsty's request was just the type of challenge he relished. The search for inspiration led him out into the garage where he stored a stack of old sketch pads, some going back to when he was at secondary school. He ended up sitting on the floor, going through them one by one. At some point Danny joined him.

"If you see anything," he instructed Danny, "with stars or ships or whales or such like, let me have a look-see."

"No problem, Dad!"

There must have been about forty sketch books. Some of the older ones were tatty, the seams falling apart or the inks faded. The search had a refreshing effect. Like looking through old family photo albums.

"And," said Danny in a mock bow, "how about this one, Mr Jennings?"

Dexter held the sketch out. "Aha! I think this is exactly what we're looking for."

"Shame it is sellotaped in half but it's got everything you asked for, doesn't it, Dad?"

Dexter remembered the day he had drawn it. One Sunday afternoon, the family had been watching Jumanji on video while he was behind them at the dining room table drawing the picture he was now looking at. Despite his mother's pleas to leave him be, his father had kept asking him to put down his pens and join the family. Finally, his father had sunk down the rest of his lager and, much to the consternation of the family, paused the film.

"What is it supposed to be?" he asked, snatching the picture from the table.

"Isn't it obvious?"

"Watch your tongue, boy." His father had deliberately made a show of not recognising anything in the picture.

"Looks like nonsense to me, Dexter. What do you think?" He'd held it up for the rest of them to see.

"Looks like a giant bubble over the sea," said his older brother, Phillip. He'd been the swot; homework always done on time, A's and A Stars in every exam.

"No, it's a ball, bouncing on water." This had come from his younger brother, Jake. Jake was the sportsman. No good at schoolwork, Jake had been a skilled left winger on the football pitch and could run a hundred metres in less than fifteen seconds. His father had also been good at sports at school and had often reminded his family that he'd made the County Finals twenty-five years before.

Dexter had only been good at one thing: art. He loved to draw. He loved to paint. He was happy with either brush or pencil but excelled with ink. On parents' evening, his art teacher had said he was certainly a candidate for Art School. His father had laughed out loud at this suggestion.

How, he had been desperate to know, did anyone make a living from drawing? The teacher had begun to list a few possibilities which had been wasted on his father who, shaking his head, had moved onto the Maths table.

"It's a hot air balloon floating over an old sailing boat," he'd told his dad.

"Ah, I can see it now, but I think you've made it too fancy. It's like two pictures mixed up in one."

With that, he'd torn the picture into two halves, separating the balloon from the boat. "That's much better. Don't you agree?" He'd held up the two halves and everyone, his mother included, had nodded their heads in agreement, anxious to return to the film. "Now, Dexter, come and join us."

Dexter had later sellotaped the picture back together and placed it in a plastic file. He'd cursed his father until he fell asleep, but his father had won the day. Art school, and any of the careers mentioned by the teacher, were never spoken of again. He'd left school with few qualifications, the only one of note was the A in art. He'd gone straight from school to work in a mechanic's yard.

He'd soon discovered that he didn't have any talent at that and had often been relegated to mundane jobs such as cleaning up, polishing, sweeping. It wasn't until a couple of years later that he'd found a way forward. He'd been doodling on a receipt book during his break when one of the workers had come in. Admiring the drawing of a hooked Arabic dagger with a decorated handle, he'd said, "If I were to have a tattoo, this would be it." The idea had stuck. It had taken him another year before he was accepted as an apprentice to the famous tattooist, Rave Crooker.

When Thirsty Kirsty returned the following week, she was greeted with an ink drawing of some hot air balloons floating in a starry sky, a sailing boat on the waves below and, wanting to tick all the boxes, a blue whale swam beneath the sea.

"You are a genius," Kirsty said. "It's like you have got into my brain and found exactly what I wanted."

It took two sessions and over six hours, but Kirsty ended up with a work of art on her right thigh that she was excited to show others.

When Dexter was making the final touches and on the back of some of their conversation, Kirsty mentioned a group she was a member of.

"It's all about QAnon. Such a relief being with others who share the same beliefs. Mind-blowing stuff. Fancy coming along?"

Ursula

Why she had volunteered to set up a local writing group, Ursula couldn't quite fathom.

She had sensed that her 'gang' of women had become tired of meeting up for coffee. They had wanted more. They'd been both elevated and burdened by their experiences; all had dabbled with the written word as a means to unchain the past by attempting capture of the present. Be it fear of commitment or dread of arrogance, not one of them had taken the plunge until Ursula had asked in her best matter-of-fact deadpan voice whether they were going to 'do this thing or not'. They had uniformly nodded their heads in agreement.

"Okay, ladies, let's go for the Budmouth Writing Circle." When she'd added the suggestion that, for the time being, she would be chair of the Circle, their relief had turned into a flurry of praise and gratitude.

"First meeting will be the first Friday morning next month, 10am in one of the library rooms."

Brenda had waved her little hand for attention. "Do you think Writing Group would be more suitable?" Brenda was very good at introducing red herrings at the last minute but Ursula had learnt how to shut her up.

"Excellent idea," she'd agreed through gritted teeth. "Circle, group, triangle, association or band—no odds to me."

Brenda had been predictably taken aback that she may have to be responsible for an actual decision.

"On second thoughts, I think we should stick with Writing Circle."

On the morning of the inaugural meeting, much to the bewilderment of the dogs, Ursula set the alarm and was out walking the beach by seven o'clock. It was a spring tide, even though they were already into the autumn; the sea was still shallow a mile out. As usual, she gave herself the task of describing the sea. A watery carpet laced with ripples too tired to make a splash. Not that good, she admitted. Or, making herself laugh: a snot-green pool of feathers and shells so shallow, even a rodent would be safe from drowning!

As soon as the dogs were off their leads, they dashed around like it was the first time they had been there. Ahmed was straight into the water looking for an imaginary stone. Carlo kept well away from the sea, he was more interested in a ball being repeatedly thrown and retrieved. Fair enough, he was a dog after all, but he was back with it in twenty seconds and yelping for another lob. Desmond, good old faithful Desmond, lumbered along beside her, stopping occasionally to roll in the sand.

The new novel was progressing satisfactorily. The accompanying feeling it gave her made her shine inside and was nothing short of euphoric. She felt something grand and significant and portentous was taking place. More than anything, she was enjoying herself. It was one huge celebration of herself—of Ursula Bird. She was currently at a crucial point. She had described the months of torture and torment at Robert's hands. She had cried all over again at the book fayre scene but mostly at the killing of Rossetti. That, essentially, was the moment that had finally turned her.

A strange peace had come over her that night, replacing the horror of it all. She had known there and then where this serenity had come from. She'd known Robert was scum and that his own malicious venom would end up poisoning him. To know in her gut that Robert was a dead man walking had filled her with a calmness she hadn't felt since the day before he had moved into her place. She had to acknowledge that to write her story was delivering a joy close to sexual pleasure.

By virtue of their habits, a targeted victim inadvertently provides the potential assailant with perfect opportunities to plan the ultimate intervention. Robert had his personal litany of routine. Ursula had begun making notes. Alcohol was commonly involved and she had known this would be an ideal lubricant to facilitate his demise. Friday nights had been the nights he'd always savoured as the climax of the week. There had been absolutely no reason for this at all, because he'd only worked three nights a week in a local supermarket. Because he'd been living with her basically rent-free, he hadn't needed much cash, so he'd found working nights gave him the maximum money for the minimum input.

What she'd actually longed to do was to pierce his skull with an ice pick—just like what had happened to Leon Trotsky. Ursula had known this wasn't a particularly good idea. Being a practical person, she'd thought of the mess of blood. She'd pondered on the ensuing chaos with the dogs and she'd wondered what she would do if the one blow was not enough and the great oaf chased her around the house, zombie-like, with the implement still sticking out of his head. Also, she would lose her freedom, which had roughly translated to him winning, and her and the dogs losing. Her freedom was too high a price to pay for his murder. No, the best thing was to engineer an unfortunate accident.

After his drinking sessions, Robert was always extremely clumsy and ham-fisted. He hadn't needed anybody's help to fall over. It had dawned on her that what she needed to do was to capitalise on the wonderful combination of his alcohol-fuelled bungling with the reassuring force of gravity. She'd begun setting her trap, and the trap was her house, and her house had become an unnervingly unsafe place to be for a drunken bastard such as Robert Greening.

At ten o'clock, Ursula was sitting in the library with Brenda. "Maybe, a circle was too ambitious a title. Maybe, a writing duet would have been more appropriate?"

By ten past, people started drifting in and by the half hour, there were seven of them.

"I'm hoping this will be the last time I have to make this introduction. Welcome all. This is the first meeting of the Budmouth Writing Circle."

She was halfway through her explanation of the format when none other than Greg Andrews popped his head round the door. His sorrys for being late cut no ice with Ursula and she continued without acknowledging his appearance.

Two hours later and she was quite surprised at how much they had accomplished. When Harris brought up politics and started complaining about the unpatriotic remainers, Ursula was quick to rebuff him and return to the task in hand. Every participant was given the chance to introduce themselves and make a few comments on their writing careers. When Ruby decided to tell her whole life story, Ursula skilfully interrupted her at 1973, thanked her and politely asked the next person to contribute.

Afterwards they chose a random subject — Loose Ends — and each disappeared into their own thought cocoon to scribble away in silence for thirty minutes. Each of them were then invited to read their creations out loud. With a few dodgy exceptions, the standard was reasonably good.

Ursula pulled it all back together at the end, made a few intelligent comments and hoped that she would see them all in two weeks' time.

Matthew

It was a perfectly reasonable request for Joy to be buried back in Ely in Cambridgeshire, where she was born and brought up. However, come the anniversary of her death or her birthday or the date of their wedding, it was almost impossible getting up there. Whether by car, coach or train, the journey was cumbersome and laborious and often necessitated an overnight stay.

With apologies to Joy, he'd given up trying ten years ago. Instead, he'd arranged to have a small patch in his garden cornered off. An arched trellis of clematis, Joy's favourite, led to a small bench which overlooked a stone plaque fringed with primroses.

Joy Mary Price 1946 – 1997
We shall not cease from exploration.

After she'd died, he'd made what in hindsight was a terrible mistake; he'd rushed back to work. He had thought that was the best way to cope with bereavement. The pain was unendurable. He'd kept seeing her everywhere, hearing her voice, waiting for her to sneak up behind him and put her arms around him and kiss his cheek.

As part of his job, many times he had quoted C.S. Lewis's words on grief to others: *'No one ever told me that grief felt so like fear'*.

When Joy had died, he'd found out what the words truly meant. A fear had ripped him open and infected every cell of his body. It was an insidious terror which had invaded his every sense. He could hardly think. Even when he had been attempting to read something, panic had shaken him awake, the words swarming on the page like wasps. Time on his own had served as a cruel reminder of his loss. He had made an early decision to get back to normal as soon after the funeral as he could. Surely throwing himself into helping others was an excellent way in which to channel his energies and placate his grief?

It had worked for about four months. Then he'd begun to notice what he would later describe as an absence of self.

In a sermon, he would lose his way and end up fudging his way through it with platitudes. Usually top-notch for remembering names, he'd kept forgetting the names of people who he had known for years. On one occasion, he had been introducing a new member of the parish to his verger and, for the life of him, he couldn't think of his name. The verger had been visibly irritated at having to cut in and introduce himself.

The turning point had been when he had found himself on the cliffs at Church Ope, gazing out to sea. Coming to, he was shaking in the bitter breeze. He had obviously been there for some time and yet had no recollection as to how he had got there. It was the bishop who had eventually approached him, not the other way around. He had suggested a month off for a period of reflection.

The period of reflection had lasted for six months. He had been so resistant to agree to even a day of reflection but as soon as he'd acquiesced, it was as if the dam he had constructed to hold back his grief had suddenly broken and every part of him had been lost in its flood.

Though hardly registering with him, locals had helped him out, gone shopping for him and cleaned the house. Eventually, in the light of everyone's insistence, he'd been to the doctors, but he'd refused antidepressants.

"Whatever I have to feel, I want to feel. I don't want to be shielded from my pain."

He had agreed to sleeping pills. Nights were unbearable if he couldn't sleep. He'd told Dr Michaels that a sleepless night was like getting into his own coffin but he was still alive and longing for daylight. Knocking himself out had helped.

"Ah, there you are." It was his neighbour, Eddie, leaning over the fence. "For one minute I thought you had gone on one of your walkabouts."

"Cheeky! Been here all the time. It's the anniversary," he said, nodding towards the plaque.

"Oh, I'm sorry matey."

"Nothing to be sorry for," he said. "It would have been her birthday."

"Happy birthday, Joy," Eddie said, taking off his cap. "Tell you what, I was just about to make myself a brew. Fancy one?"

"That would be splendid, Eddie." Matthew paused, lost in thought. "I didn't go into a church once, not once." He found himself speaking aloud, Eddie sitting next to him.

"Is that a fact?" Eddie said, not sure what his friend was talking about.

"In all those months after Joy died, I didn't so much as set one foot in church."

"Each to his own, I suppose."

"And when I did go back, you know what occurred to me?"

"Can't say I do."

"It was a holy communion. There we were, repeating the same words I had been saying those months before and the same words I had been saying since I joined the cloth and the same words I used to mumble as a choirboy."

"What you trying to get at?"

"Here we were, spouting out the same old stuff week in, week out. What came to me is that if there is a God, he must be a lover of both routine and repetition. In other words, a complete and utter old fart. Or he must be bored stupid. We talk about the living God but either he's gone AWOL or he's in some sort of coma."

"That would have got you burnt at a stake in the old days."

The two friends fell into silence, finishing their mugs of tea.

"That's T.S. Elliot that quote," Matthew pointed out. *"The Four Quartets* were her favourite verse,"

"Never heard of her."

"It's a him, actually"

At six, Fiona popped around with his dinner. He liked to sit down to watch the news, his dinner on a cushioned tray on his lap.

"How was it today?"

"All good, thank you."

"I bumped into Tia in town. My goodness, I haven't seen such a transformation in a person. The first time you introduced me to her I thought she looked like a little waif. Well, not anymore. Her interview is next week."

"Interview?"

"For the nurse training, silly."

"Thank you for reminding me, Fiona. I'll order some flowers."

Tia

And here she was, Tia Hearn—single mum of two, a small-town girl, a benefit slut, a no-hoper, a millennium kid, Generation Y, twenty-three years old—sitting in a lecture theatre, waiting for Dr Alana Wycombe to deliver an overview of the course entitled, 'What it takes to become a Nurse'.

Getting there on time had been a logistical nightmare; Nara was actually up before she was. She'd entered her bedroom with a cup of tea and a handmade card, a heart of her red lipstick on the front: *Good luck today Mummy, Kojo and me Nara are very prowd of you xxx.*

Tears and hugs had to be quickly followed by a shower. Waking Kojo up for an instant breakfast had come next. Once everyone was dressed they'd stood around waiting for the neighbour to pick Nara up. Despite reminders, her mum was ten minutes late to collect Kojo for the day.

When she'd boarded the train and sat down, it had dawned on her that she had hardly ever been on a train and never on her own. How did one act?

Watching others come on and sit down had been an education. Some had fiddled around with their luggage or in their bags. Some had immediately started consuming sandwiches or drinks. Others had got out notebooks, books or papers or plugged in earphones.

One girl had sat in front of a propped mirror applying lipstick and eyeliner. Tia's conclusion: you act as if nobody else was there — everyone together and yet each alone.

Entering the lecture theatre had been equivalent to entering an ancient temple or a mediaeval cathedral. Hugging her briefcase to her chest, she had stood there in absolute awe, in total reverence. When the other students had arrived and begun searching for a seat, she'd smiled to herself. Ah, it's just like the train: act as if nobody else was there.

Dr Wycombe liked a joke and was making every effort to put the new intake at ease. Her PowerPoint presentation was crammed with cartoons — a doubting face becoming a tearful face becoming a smiling face, nurses chasing patients, doctors reprimanding nurses. It was working. The new students became relaxed. The girl next to her whispered a hiya to Tia. Her name was Suzi with an i.

Technically, Tia shouldn't have been there. She had failed her interview. It had been the second slot in the afternoon, but they'd been running late.

Through the glass door, she'd heard the mumbles of the questioning panel followed by the deadpan responses of the interviewee. Tia had been through her phone many times already. She was aware that Teresa May was in crisis from members of her own party. Trump was up to his old tricks, harping on about the building of the Wall across the USA's southern border. And someone was murdered by someone else somewhere.

Her nerves had been getting the better of her. Perhaps her dad had been right when he'd said she wasn't nursing material, they needed nurses with good qualifications. Level C in Domestic Science wouldn't cut it.

"Anyways," he'd concluded, "you've those two tykes to think about. Don't get it in your head we're going to look after the blighters." Her mum had been positive and encouraging but she could only hear her dad's voice in her head. She'd sighed and was about to pick up her bag and leave when Louise had sent through a gif of a girl twirling in a dress shouting *you can do it, bitch!*

The door had opened on cue and a man, beaming from ear to ear had emerged.

Her first thought had been that he was a smug bastard but he'd mouthed good luck to her and she'd changed her mind.

There were three of them; two women and a man. When they'd introduced themselves, Tia hadn't heard a word and had wondered if she'd suddenly gone deaf. She hadn't been sure where to put her bag.

"The first thing I am duty bound to say, Tia — may we call you Tia? — is that you don't appear to have enough points to qualify as a nursing student."

"Why was I offered an interview then?"

The man had looked at the woman to his left who'd shrugged.

"We don't actually process the applications. It must be an error."

She'd had to try hard not to burst into tears. Why bother? *Hardly nursing material.*

"But," the man had said, quickly realising his bluntness, "as you are here, tell us why you want to become a nurse."

She was back out on the seat she had been waiting on before. It felt like she'd been in there for hours, babbling away, losing her thread, skipping words, even letting out a swear word.

Not nursing material.

She'd looked at her watch. She had been in that room for a short fifteen minutes.

She'd found the cafe, ordered a double espresso, then found the smoking area and blindly chain smoked. Every question they'd asked her she'd then answered in her head. She'd appreciated that they hadn't been deliberately obtrusive, as she had thought at the time, but had been trying to facilitate her thinking. She had fucked up big time. She'd pictured telling everyone the sad news. Louise and her Mum, Matthew and Fiona, all wearing their sorry faces while her father stood behind them smirking.

A couple of hours had passed before she'd woken up from the trap she'd so willingly fallen into. She must have smoked twenty cigarettes. The cafe had emptied and filled and emptied again during the time she had been sitting there. Emerging back into the day, she'd found the foyer crowded with passing groups of people all chatting happily away.

Once outside, she'd been surprised to see the chair of the panel, his tie undone, smoking a cigarette. Tia had frozen, taken a deep breath and marched up to him.

"This is what I can bring to nursing. This is why you are going to accept me on your course."

She'd told him everything. Well, not everything, not about her mistakes or her dad or her failed past but she'd told him about her; everything about herself, about Tia. Though taken aback at this sudden onslaught, he'd listened to what she had to say.

Two days later she'd had an acceptance letter from the university, scribbled on the bottom was a note saying thank you for drawing to our attention the qualifications you omitted in your original application.

"And then we have the assignments ..." Dr Wycombe pointedly pressed the button and to everybody's amusement, a cartoon appeared of a perspiring student swimming in a sea of papers and books. "All our deadlines are generous, but when they are due in, they are due in. The date is set and the time is always 10am. A minute later and it will be regarded as a non-submission. You may be granted an extension but the reasons have to be specific, evidenced and agreed beforehand. For example, when it comes to excuses we're talking being recently resuscitated, tsunamis, revolution, the second coming or the death of your favourite hamster."

"What if you finish the assignment early?" Tia was surprised to hear anyone speak in such a crowded room. It was even more of a surprise to discover that the speaker was one Tia Hearn.

"Ha! I see we have an ambitious student."

"Sorry, was that a silly question?"

"No question is silly. If you submit the assignment the day after it is set, well, good for you but I'm afraid you don't get any extra marks. You will find some essays you will be able to rattle off without a problem. Others will feel like the twelve trials of Hercules. All you have to keep in mind is that deadline."

At the end of the session, Dr Wycombe made one last comment as she was packing her things away.

"By the way, all those excuses I listed for late assignments are valid, except for the death of your hamster. Get your assignments in by the deadline we give you. You can grieve for your hamster in your own time."

As they were drinking wine later, she must have repeated the hamster joke about five times. But Louise didn't mind. This was the first time she had seen Tia this happy.

CHAPTER 6
April 2019

Global Strike for Climate involves over 1.6 million people from 125 countries.

Extinction Rebellion blocks central London with a massive protest.

Theresa May is defeated again in the Commons on her proposed deal with Europe.

Trump and vice-president Pence speak at the National Rifle Association's Convention.

Jon

When Jon first woke up, he had to remind himself again where he was. It took him a few seconds before his brave new world fell into place. His entire wardrobe was lying in a pile on a chair. The tap was still dripping. Initially it had kept him awake and then eventually it had sent him to sleep. His must-have books were scattered on the smallest dining table ever made. The rest to follow later. The wicker chair was cluttered with toiletries. The whole scene was Van Gogh's bedroom at Arles but drained of colour.

Still comatose in bed, he lit a cigarette, breaking one of the Ten Rules of Living Here pinned in large font on the back of the door. This mundane version of the Ten Commandments included dictums on not having pets, keeping certain hours quiet, maximum decibels, garbage, guests and the polite request that showers should not last any longer than fifteen minutes.

This was not quite what Jon had in mind when he'd decided to make a stand against the injustices which had befallen him. He had expected Lynda to change her tack.

Their previous agreement had suited the both of them and had worked effectively for years. Her falling in love was spoiling things.

He'd reminded her that he had fallen in love with Esme Holt but he hadn't let that mess up the status quo. Then there had been the problem of the children; their home. Maybe this was not such a big quandary for Victoria as she had applied to Bristol University but Sophie was only nine or ten years old—he was always a year behind or in front. That Lynda retained the house was an unspoken assumption which, only later, Jon wished he had questioned.

As for his fucking university, they had shot themselves in the foot. He had seen his course through, taken his sabbatical, written his soon-to-be published paper and waited for them to grovel to him with a plan to install him back onto the team. But they had never come. In a bid to punish them for their arrogance, he had resigned. The only reaction he had received was a letter thanking him for his unique contribution to university life. It had come with a twenty-five pound Marks and Spencer's voucher inside a little card signed by Helen Elliot wishing him all the very best.

Unfortunately, he had met Ian Tait in a pub perhaps a week after. The git couldn't get that smug smile off his face and Jon had left the whisky Tait had bought him standing on the bar. The incident had infuriated him; being insulted by a tit like Tait was the ultimate affront. He had made a snap decision to leave, to get out of Southampton and start up somewhere new, different, unusual. He had driven to the sleepy town of Christchurch in Dorset, and as a temporary refuge, had signed a six-month lease on a small studio flat near the priory.

In the following months he had enjoyed numerous odd moments contemplating how he had made such a huge resolution on the back of a whimsy. To trace the source of his decision was almost impossible but he had added countless justifications after the event.

It was gone twelve before Jon struggled out of bed and threw on some tatty clothes. Jogging trousers, T-shirts and trainers had become his new uniform. Although he kept drifting off into a sort of thoughtfulness (minus the thoughts), he cajoled himself along.

In a twee English way, Christchurch was undoubtedly beautiful. Hemmed in by two rivers, the Avon and the lesser Stour, it had its history: a Norman Castle, the ancient mill, the harbour estuary and the priory presiding over it all. His walk ended up in Ye Olde George where he washed down his lunch with a few pints. Arriving back at the flat, he was greeted by the landlord's son, Ben. He had been living there for over a month and already Ben had called in several times, always for some spurious reason.

"Just checking you are okay."

"Like last week, no complaints so far."

"Apologies but I forgot to ask for the £10 deposit for the key. Well, it's twenty actually as you have two."

Jon couldn't recall a key deposit being referred to in either the Ten Rules or the lease but he wasn't going to make a fuss. Ben followed him into the flat without being invited.

"Still got some unpacking to do, I see."

Jon rifled in his jacket pocket and found a handful of cash. "Alright in coins?"

"Money is money." Jon counted it out into his hand.

"How's the book going?" Ben asked, looking around the messy room.

"Slowly."

Ben was at the door and about to leave. "You look like an active guy," he said with a wink. "I'm just on my way to our Weymouth properties. I have an arrangement with a couple of our female tenants and wonder if you would like to join me?"

"Arrangement?"

"An understanding — a bit of give and take, if you get my drift?"

This was the amateur talking to the professional. Jon definitely got his drift. It was Jon's turn to look around the room, focusing on the unopened laptop.

"Why not?"

Jon had visited Weymouth but had put it down as a seaside destination for rabble who could not afford to travel abroad. Entering along the beach road, the curve of sand fringed by beach huts, cafes and amusements, came as no surprise.

"George the third came here thirteen times. Queen Victoria came once."

"She obviously had a bit more sense."

"Glad to say that this is a Brexit town too — just like Christchurch."

"I could have guessed that."

Ben turned into a side street and drew up outside a three-story building.

"Believe it or not, we managed to cram four lettings into this place. You're going to love number two. Come and have a look."

Ben went through the front door with Jon following. On the ground floor there were two dwellings and a narrow stairwell which led upstairs to the other two flats. Ben nodded towards number one.

"The one that lived there was a real treat. Shame she moved out."

Jon saw a pile of letters on the windowsill addressed to Tia Hearn.

The door to number two eventually opened; a woman answered. Seeing it was Ben, she opened the door for him to enter.

"I've brought a friend."

She hardly looked up. She must have been about thirty. She was so thin, Jon wondered if she had an eating disorder.

"Which one's first?"

They slammed the bedroom door shut, leaving Jon sitting on the smelly sofa, which he shared with a bundle of washing. The same Ten Rules he had stuck to his door was stuck to hers but going by the stench in the room, she was definitely breaking the ones on cigarettes and drugs.

A few photographs were arranged on the mantelpiece above the two-bar electric heater. One was obviously the woman he had just met, but younger, happier, holding a baby boy, of whom there was no evidence of living here.

He heard mumbled words from the other room but one word was clear: slut.

It was a blessing to get out of the flat and find himself on the seafront. He apparently had a limit to his decadence. The wind had picked up and he welcomed the feeling that it was blowing straight through him. A woman with three dogs passed him and nodded a hello. Two dogs were behaving but she had to keep calling for the third. Carlos couldn't resist running in and out of the water. He watched her walk the length of the sands and then head back. Passing him again she asked if he was alright.

"Do you have somewhere to go to tonight?"

"Sub divo."

"Ha! Haven't heard that phrase since Grammar School. Under the wide-open sky."

Lexi

Some days held more weight than others. Some days became tipping points whereby life was never the same as it was the day before. Many days dragged their feet; seconds became minutes, minutes became hours. Other days flew by; it was difficult to catch your breath, and they seemed to have no purpose other than to rush to the day that followed. Sometimes though, those rare days came along. Maybe they were the accumulation of unresolved longing or the innate compulsion to nudge life in a different direction. Today was such a day.

Lexi had prevaricated, excused or blotted out the fact that, after nearly three years of illness, she was ready to return to school. Despite being absolutely desperate to get her life back on track, she was consumed with a terrible apathy; a grave impatience to stay unwell, to remain disabled, bedridden, hidden.

The previous evening, she had actually prayed that the shadow would return to her room, sneak in at night and pierce her being to its core. She had quickly substituted it with another prayer — that nothing would happen, she would be fine and wake up full of life and ready for action. Her anxiety was natural enough. She had missed out on so much schooling. Yes, the school had regularly dropped off work for her, her parents did what they could and she had the internet, zoom and YouTube as surrogate teachers. One of her favourite courses, if you could call it that, had been provided through her great Aunt Ursula.

Her aunt had directed her attention to literature and poetry in a way which had made it come alive. Ursula had told her to read a poem or a passage and then would simply ask her what she had seen? Not what she had read or heard or felt, what she had seen.

The day arrived. A good sign: she woke up with the alarm and not before. A good sign: her mother didn't bounce in trying to dress or organise her. A good sign: the rain of the last few days had vanished and the sun was throwing her bedroom into brilliant clarity.

Okay, one thing at a time, no rush, as her dad always said, no rush, just direction.

Face facts, it was going to be hard. She was in the sixth form. The usual application procedure had been shelved in favour of course work, as she had missed her GCSEs. Lexi had to sit at least six this year. No pressure.

On top of that, she was studying English and Psychology A levels. This would be a busy year for her.

Rayn, who was two terms into the drama course, would meet her at the gate. Lexi texted her: *See you in an hour. In the meantime read The Way It Is by Lyn Ungar. Read it now!*

Lexi had actually read out the poem to her months ago when Rayn had managed to procure several mini cans of cocktails. It had started them both off. Rayn called her a shit for making her cry. The urgent *'Now!'* had become their standard go-to joke, replicating the time when Lexi had phoned her parents and told them to get their arses up those stairs to her daughter.

And that the pit of unfulfilled longing in your heart
had gradually, and without your really noticing,
been filled in — patched like a pothole, not quite
the same as it was, but good enough.

The family had prepared for when Lexi entered the kitchen, ready for the day ahead. Both brother and sister were eating their breakfast quietly, mum and dad leaning against adjacent sides, drinking coffee. They turned and looked at her.

"Guess what? I'm going back to school."

It was silent at first until Sarah started to clap, the rest of the family joining in with hoots and hurrahs.

The school was smaller than she remembered it; less grand, less daunting, if not a little scruffier. Rayn was there as planned, chatting away as if nothing was happening at all: no absence, no illness, no suicide attempt. Rayn was buzzing. A piece she had written for the blog, *And don't talk to me about Emotions*, had basically gone viral overnight.

"I thought it was shit but apparently not!"

The last time she had been in a class there had been over thirty of them. In the A level English class there were only eleven; eight girls and three boys. The teacher was new to her. Mrs Grenwood introduced herself as a literary nerd. Before they made a start on the work, Mrs Grenwood, with the help of the students, cleared the surplus desks away to the side and placed their desks in a semicircle with her at the centre.

"Four events," she explained, "that made me nerdy about English. One poem, one short story and two novels. The poem was DH Lawrence's *The Ship of Death*. The short story was *Metamorphosis* by Kafka. The first novel was the *The Bridge of San Luis Rey* by an American Writer, Thornton Wilder. The second novel, though unpublished, was the work of my own teacher, Carol Prescott. It was a great read about a priest who had turned to crime to help the poorest of his parishioners out. All four opened my mind up to the creative possibilities of the written word. You obviously wouldn't have heard of Carol but has anyone heard of any of the others I mentioned?"

The boy next to Lexi said he knew the first two authors but had not read the pieces she mentioned.

"Well, ladies and gentlemen, we have plenty of time to crack open those particular treasure troves. By way of starting us off, think about what has brought you here. Any particular works of art? Any odd bits of literature? Or, maybe, it was a film, a graphic novel, an idea, notion or someone you admire, either in your personal life or in the world of letters. Take your time. Just write about what influenced your interest."

Lexi wrote in her file, *The Mirror* by Sylvia Plath. The boy next to her looked over.

"Cool," he said, smiling, his blue eyes looking directly into her. And she realised that a new life had begun for her and, from now on, everything would be different.

Dexter

"Tell me the last time we did this?"

They were lying in bed, Dee cuddling into Dexter. The boys could be heard playing in the lounge. Renting a log cabin on the hill above Lyme Regis, they had decided to get away for a long weekend. Whether they were thirty miles away or thirty thousand made no difference. The important thing was that they were on a mini-holiday, the first time for four years.

"We must make sure we do this more often," agreed Dexter

"Hell yes! From now on, at least once every year."

They laid like this for another half an hour.

"Have you ever thought about having another child, Dext? You always wanted a little girl, didn't you?"

"Wow! Where's this come from?"

"Being away from the old routine," she said, putting her hand on his cock, "it's just got me thinking, that's all."

"Well," said Dexter, turning towards her, "No time like the present, as they say." Before their first kiss ended, Danny tapped lightly on the door.

"And that was that, as they also say!"

"Typical," she said with a chuckle. "Tell you what, Dext, you take them down to Lyme. I didn't sleep that well—never do in a strange bed. But you go and have some quality dad-kids time."

"You sure?"

"Totally sure," she said, snuggling back into the bed.

Dexter could have walked down to the town with the boys but decided to take the car, parking next to the beach.

"Right, lads, the first thing we must do is walk to the end of the cobb."

Anyone would think he had announced they had won the lottery, the boys were that excited. The tide was out, leaving the sandy beach exposed but the ancient cobb sketched into the blue translucent water like a protective arm.

"So, why's it called a cobb and not a regular pier?"

"No idea Andrew. My guess would be that it's made of cobblestones."

They stood on the very end of the cobb, the channel spanning out to the south, the little promenade with its willy-nilly shoreline of houses to the north.

"I am definitely going to live here for a year when I grow up," Danny announced.

"You're so lame," retorted Andrew. Everything was lame at the moment. Lame or sweet. Andrew was working on a new image. He looked over to the woodland and the clay cliffs, the same cliffs where fossils are commonly found, the place where Mary Anning had found the marine dinosaur with the unpronounceable name.

Andrew thought about mentioning it but resisted the urge, unsure as to how his father would react. He hadn't mentioned any of his beliefs for some time but Andrew didn't want to take the risk.

His father, meanwhile, was also looking in the same direction. It was oh-so tempting to put the boys right on the dinosaurs. Going by the trash books which they were bringing home from school, they were being given the usual sugar-coated lies which had been trotted out for decades. Of course, he didn't believe that the fossils were planted by the devil to fool Christians. That was obvious nonsense but what he was learning about the Masonic Order was of a more worrying nature. Dinosaurs are used to tie their own ideas of evolution together or to make money from. His boys really needed to know this stuff but a promise was a promise and he bit his lip.

On the esplanade, Dexter sent the boys to get themselves an ice cream while he caught up on the latest on the Dorset-Anon site on his phone.

Queuing, the boys were ahead of four girls who were giggling over some joke one of them, a girl with purple hair, had just told. Despite the girls being much older—a few years difference at this age is formidable—Andrew and his younger brother went quiet. They couldn't conceal their interest, glancing back as naturally as possible when they could.

Walking away, Danny was about to take his first lick when, from nowhere, a seagull with hawk-like agility flew down, turned almost ninety degrees and took the top of his Rum and Raisin ice cream. After a moment of disbelief, everybody around started laughing, including Andrew. But not Danny. Danny was left looking at the empty cone. He threw it down in disgust, another seagull immediately swooping down opportunistically.

"Don't worry, let's go and get some more money from Dad."

But as they were walking across the esplanade, the girl with purple hair tapped Danny on the back and presented him with a new ice cream.

"I didn't know what you liked so I got you chocolate chip."

"My favourite," Danny lied. As the other three caught up, it was Andrew's turn to wish his ice cream had been taken by a gull.

"You down here on holiday?"

"Yes, that's our dad there," said Danny, always more comfortable talking to strangers than Andrew was. "How about you?"

"No, we live here for our sins."

"Your sins couldn't have been that bad living here." Danny had stolen his line.

"We're Rayn, Molly, Carla and this is the famous Lexi."

"Andrew and Danny," Andrew was so glad to hear the sound of his own voice. "Why you famous?"

"Ah," said Rayn, drawing her friend towards her, "she just is."

Andrew noticed that the famous Lexi was relatively skinny and walked with a slight limp.

Now back with Dexter, who was somewhat taken back by the addition of four young women, Danny told him the story of the snatched ice cream.

"Thank you, ladies, that's very kind of you."

Lexi could not help seeing the screen Dexter had been scrolling through on his phone. "I check out those idiots too every now and then. You can't fight what you don't understand."

Five minutes later, and much to the boys' annoyance, they were in the car and driving back to the cabin. Dexter had failed to pick up their interest in meeting up with some new potential friends but they both understood why their dad had suddenly whisked them off. He had been caught out.

As soon as they were back, all three slammed the car doors for their own reasons and marched into the log cabin.

"Dad's starting again, Mum." Andrew, frustrated still by the image of the four girls, couldn't stop himself from announcing his irritation. Nothing more had to be said, Dee knew exactly what her son was referring to.

Andrew wished he had kept his mouth shut. After a few drinks, husband and wife started to argue, Dee reminding him that he had promised and had agreed to the consequences of any breach. Dexter denied any involvement whilst leaking little parcels of information which confirmed the opposite. Dee was trying to be reasonable but in the end, exploded saying that he had been warned. He had been warned!

Dexter, realising his game was up, stood up and searching for ammunition, came up with, "and don't think we're having another kid, because that's the last thing that's going to happen."

Registering his words, Dee was flabbergasted that he had mentioned this at all, especially in front of the boys.

"And if we did, we wouldn't get her vaccinated like these two here." As soon as the words were uttered, he knew he had gone too far.

"Please get out, Dexter," Dee said, suddenly as sober as a judge. "Don't come back tonight. I don't care what you do or where you go, just don't come back tonight."

Ursula

Of all places, Ursula was meeting Greg in a pub. She had wanted to tell him it was a meeting, not a date, but when she discovered the staff had reserved the fireside seat in the Red Lion she reined herself in. Finding herself in this ridiculous situation was, after all, her own silly fault.

Let's organise a poetry competition for Dorset youngsters under the age of twenty-five. Bad idea. Talk about giving yourself a hard time. Ursula had half-hoped the group would dismiss the notion as evidence of her contrary nature. Unfortunately, they had loved it. With such a scheme had come a tsunami of decision-making: prize money, incentives, advertising, judging, to mention but a few. Wind on a few months and they were wading through the three-thousand and twenty-two submissions. They had anticipated several hundred. They'd regretted not setting the limit of entries per person to two rather than five. The group had managed to persuade the local Lions group to cough up £1000 for prize money; £500 for the winner, £200 for second, a hundred for the third and £50 for each four highly commended.

Ursula was quite aware that sometimes she could open her mouth before thinking something through but at their first November meeting, she had stopped herself blurting out that the average age must be around or above pension age. In all their meetings so far there had been three people who were under thirty. They must have felt they had entered a twilight zone of literary oldies.

Nick had a mental health problem and only came for two weeks. He was obviously gifted and came up with what Ursula thought was a brilliant line: *I stopped believing in belief when I was eight and a half.*

Robyn, a nineteen-year-old Goth, had been caught smoking in the library toilets. She had the most interesting email address of Nolifeafterdeathrock@yahoo.com. She had lasted one session.

And there was a children's writer, Bernadette (Bernie) Serene, who, on the back of having sold a thousand copies of her first book, had thought she was there to teach them all about the written word. She made it—just—to the tea break of her first meeting.

The Submission Meetings were a mixed pleasure. Some of the poems were magical, some pure genius. To get to these gems though they'd had to wade through what Ursula called poetic bling. Of course, there had been the endless debates and, despite there being only six of them, they'd soon exposed the impassable chasms of taste, meaning and craftsmanship. For credibility purposes, the Circle had been duty-bound to offer the chair to one Jeni Swift—apparently a distant relation to Jonathan Swift. Jeni Swift had won third prize in a national poetry competition and had attracted some literary acclaim for her slim volume of verse, *Night Falls but Once*. It was Ursula's favourite joke, told several times, that if it had been any slimmer it could have come straight out of Lilliput.

They had whittled the lot down to a rump of three-hundred. At this stage, the six judges split into three groups of two. As luck would have it, Ursula had ended up paired with Greg Andrews. She had hoped for any of the others. However, Jeni was captain of this particular ship and had said she had her own undisclosed reasons for their pairing.

Ursula was already halfway through writing her novel. She had rejected her working title of *Scars make Tougher Skin* as being too self-helpy. It was consuming her in a way she had never been consumed by any writing project. She likened it to an addiction, an intense craving which she could neither stop nor limit. Sometimes, surrounded by three snoring dogs and one purring tabby, she would be scribbling away on her pads until gone three in the morning. At first, it had read like a case study. Then it had become a university thesis analysing the nature of abusive relationships. But now she knew she was hitting the right level. It was transforming into a journal of the descent into a form of madness, in which her essential self was sacrificed to the dictatorship of another.

Deciding that the only way to overthrow this tyrant she had invited into her own home, Ursula had become preoccupied, no, obsessed with his downfall. Strangely, as soon as she had made her mind up that he was a goner, she had felt she was already winning. The insurrection had started. Despite that, the intoxicated despot hadn't the slightest idea that a clock was ticking and every tick was getting ever closer to his final tock — another of her jokes.

Silence had been her first weapon. After Robert had killed Rossetti, she had withdrawn herself from him. Words had been used minimally and for convenience only. She'd ceased trying to engage, cajole or enlighten him. Taking over the spare bedroom, virtually untouched since she had moved in twenty years before, had acted as an external metaphor for her dilemma. It had been a sanctuary which had felt bizarre to her. This feeling had provided her with a strange self-consciousness, creating an inner awareness of the challenge ahead.

After his drunken binge and the subsequent slump in front of the TV, he would have to mount the stairs to empty his bladder. Occasionally he had gone outside into the yard but the dogs had thought they were in for a treat midnight walk and, much to his annoyance and her delight, they would thump their way downstairs and join him, whining and enthusiastic. If he had kicked them or sworn at them, it would have only served to harden her resolve to put an end to his pointless existence.

But how?

She'd bought some marbles and wasted a few weeks conjuring a plan. She was thinking that while he was in the loo she would sneak out, place the marbles on the top step and wait for the resultant thud. She would have to be quick, count out the marbles and retrieve every one of them before calling the ambulance. Her next plan had been to just push his carcass down the stairs but he was a fat oaf and the consequences of failure would be dire. In the end, he had provided the solution himself.

Meeting a man in a pub, let alone just going into one, was such an unusual experience for Ursula, it sent her into a panic. What to wear? Casual, casual-smart, smart-casual, or just smart? Make up or none? In the end, she literally had to face off with herself in the bathroom mirror and demand that she stopped acting like a fifteen-year-old and put on her usual jeans and jumper. She didn't have any make-up anyway.

Greg was at the fireside table, studying the top poem in the pile, when she arrived. He looked up as she entered, pulling off his reading glasses in one stroke. "What would you like to drink?"

She surprised herself by asking for a glass of wine. They agreed on a method. They would read the same poem at the same time, discuss its merits and make a decision. There would be three piles: definitely no, definitely yes and definitely maybe. Ursula assumed they would be poles apart in their judgments but discovered that, more often than not, they were in agreement.

Halfway through the process, Greg whipped off his glasses and said, "I must say, Ursula, I think it's a rare privilege to be reading these brilliant pieces. Doing so with you simply adds to the experience." He seemed pleased, if not relieved to have finally spoken his thoughts.

Ursula was uncharacteristically speechless. She sheepishly placed another poem, *Snow is rain with attitude* on the definitely yes pile.

Matthew

The last time Matthew was in the West End of London was when he had attended a conference on the challenges of modernising the church. For all intents and purposes, it had been a boring affair with a great deal on the analysis and depiction of the issues but very little on effective solutions.

He recalled the colleague sitting next to him whispering "if platitudes were the stuff of revolution, we would take over the world."

He had taken Joy along in order to make a weekend of it. That night they had gone to Les Misérables. Joy had cried at the appropriate places, whereas most of it had gone over his head.

Here he was a generation later in a crowd of marching people, chanting again and again: "Power! People! Power! People!"

Every so often, someone with a loudhailer would yell: "What do we want?"

The response would be belted out "Climate Justice."

Matthew was enjoying the buzz of solidarity. He was right in the centre, within touching distance of the pink boat *Tell the Truth*, moored smack bang on the intersection between Oxford and Regent Street. Most were younger than him but he had already come across a chap ten years his senior. In the sight of this sudden and overwhelming protest, the police were holding back, wondering what exactly could be done.

Fiona had been so angry with him for joining in with the march. Her arguments against participation had ranged from him being too old, the protesters being too aggressive, the movement being too lefty, the protest itself being unlawful and then, resorting back to her original argument, she told him that he was just too old. When all these had failed to work, she'd blamed Greta Thunberg. As Greta was too far away to blame, Fiona had fallen to criticising Tia Hearn and her part in his tomfoolery.

Matthew could put up with her objections but he couldn't extend this to Tia. "She didn't do a thing. She made me aware of what was going on in the big world. And what is going on is that this big world of ours is dying. By 2100 we will be beginning the sixth mass extinction of life."

"By 2100", she'd retorted, "you will be long-buried and forgotten. At the very most, you will be a picture in an old album and nobody will be around to remember your name."

"How cruel."

"No, stopping you from going is a kindness. Admit it, you're not strong enough for such shenanigans."

"And Fiona Willis, like you keep reminding me, I'll soon be fish food. I'm going and that is final."

He had been looking for a cause to throw himself into. After many discussions with Tia, he'd agreed with her that after the obvious demands of hunger, shelter and health, trying to save this deteriorating planet should be an overwhelming responsibility. What had tipped him into action was one of those programmes about melting ice caps. What could be more sorrowful than shots of an emaciated polar bear swimming from one lump of ice to another, searching for food increasingly out of its reach?

Needless to say, Matthew had got his way and Fiona had helped him get ready. She'd made two rounds of sandwiches and a flask of tea, and had dropped him off at the King's Statue to wait for the coach. It had been a little intimidating getting on and finding a seat but everyone was in high spirits and had greeted him like an old friend.

"Good on you, Grandad," one girl had said, winking at him.

He found the march to the centre tiring. Adrenaline levels were high though and the cacophony and the chaos of colour were lively and entertaining and drew his attention away from his discomfort.

As the day progressed, a point was reached where the police had to respond to the anarchy. Their vans drew up, parking a little away from the crowds. At first, the police kept pulling people away from around the boat, threatening them with a caution but as soon as they were released, they ran behind the police and joined the masses from the other side. A policewoman took Matthew by the arm.

"Hello," he said.

"Don't you think you're a little too old for this sort of thing?"

"Why does everyone keep going on about your age? When a thing is right, it is right, nought to do with age."

She wasn't listening. She escorted him to the pathway and ordered him to stay there. He stood there for a minute, taking in the glamour of so many people, chattering, chanting, laughing and singing.

"As I'm here …" he said to himself. He skirted the core of the crowd and wheedled his way back in from the other side. He found himself next to a family of four.

"Having a good day?" he asked the father.

"We're having a great time. We've been on several of these protests. This is by far the largest. It's an amazing turnout. How about you?"

"I'm a protest virgin, I'm afraid," he said before he realised that he had used the word virgin in front of the children.

The mother laughed at his reaction.

"Don't worry, they have heard much worse!"

The police were getting themselves organised, reaching further into the crowd and moving people on more systematically. An aggressive resistance often resulted in being dragged off into the van. Most were in festival mood and coalesced in a good-humoured way.

It was the family's turn to be escorted away from the boat. They went off as if they had just been unexpectedly invited to a party. As they were leaving and saying their goodbyes and goodlucks, the little girl turned to Matthew and said, "Be careful and watch your back."

Everyone laughed at that but Matthew was taken aback. He had seen a ghost. She looked the spitting image of Lucy Chambers, the little girl whose family he'd worked with for months when she had gone missing.

But he didn't have time to dwell on the shock because he was confronted by the same policewoman who had led him away before.

"Not you again! What's your name?"

"No Comment."

"Very funny," she said, marching him to the pavement. "Your name?"

"Told you, it's Mr N. Comment."

She rolled her eyes. "Next time, you will be arrested. Now just stay there."

He didn't, and when he did get arrested, something akin to joy flooded through him. In the back of the police van, he whispered to Joy, "Look, I've been arrested!". He could hear her warm response straight after.

"You always were a bloody fool."

Tia

Tia was desperately trying not to cry. When Sister 'invited' a student nurse into the office it was not considered to be a good sign.

Tia disappeared into the bathroom, splashed water on her face, pinched her cheeks to bring some colour back, threw a mint into her mouth, rolled it around and spat it out. This could be the end of her nursing career before it had actually begun.

How did she end up with a mentor like Sylvia Greenwich on her very first ward in Elderly Care? She knew Sylvia had taken a dislike to her on first sighting. Now she had given her the perfect excuse.

She was taking a deep breath outside the office when a fellow student nurse, Helen Vaughn, passed. Raising her eyebrows, she pressed her arm in a supportive gesture. Tia tapped as lightly on the door as she could manage.

"I can only offer you tea, coffee or water."

"Water, thank you."

"Right, Tia, as far as I can see, we have two matters to deal with. Dr Samuels and Mrs Levy. Are we in agreement?"

"Yes, Dr Samuels and Mrs Levy."

Since starting her studies Tia had found out very quickly that she'd needed to take some serious notice of the self-help tips and psychological insights she stored in her little red book of pithies. It was one thing to be titillated by these tiny gems of wisdom, it was an entirely different thing to internalise them, make sense of them and then apply them to your life.

Much to her father's gratification, the first month of her training had been an utter catastrophe. Tia had been in a spin from dawn to dusk. The children had been randomly shipped out to friends and family. When the first essay was due, Louise had turned up at seven in the morning—a time she did not ordinarily experience—and taken both children off her hands with hardly a word engaged between them.

Unusually, Nara had begun to complain, remonstrating against the crazy lack of routine. In a fit of protest, Nara had screamed out the lamentable question: why couldn't they be like a normal family?

Tia had barely been getting enough sleep either. She would find herself poring over her books into the early hours until her brain became an inanimate block of concrete. That first essay had been deleted three times before she had finally submitted it an hour before the deadline. Waiting for the mark had been pure agony. She hadn't needed to worry, as she'd got a respectable 66%. Instead of the mark reassuring her, it had set a standard she'd felt she may never achieve again.

This maddening mindset had continued until Matthew had popped in for a cup of tea. He'd found her rushing around the house, hoovering and tidying, Nara following with the duster and Kojo toddling behind.

"Tia, stop what you're doing and come and have a cup of tea."

She'd acquiesced but he could still see her mind frantically overtaking itself. When he'd asked her what was going on, Tia had started babbling away, flitting from one subject to another. Taking a deep breath, she'd finished on "and I haven't even one minute to read my red book."

"Okay," Matthew had said with a sigh, "let's start there. Where is that book of yours?"

"Right here," she'd said, pulling the tatty book out of her handbag.

"Open it up at random."
"Why?"
"Just read one out."
She'd opened it up about half way.

"I'm not afraid of death; I just don't want to be there when it happens—Woody Allen."

He'd returned her blank expression. "I think we need another one."

"I will be calm. I will be mistress of myself—Jane Austen."

"Getting closer. Surely our friend Carl Jung had something useful to say?"

It had appeared that on this occasion, he hadn't. Slightly irritated, Tia had read out one of Lao Tzu's quotes, "Nature does not hurry, yet everything is accomplished."

"Ah, finally! Right, Tia. Do you trust me?"

"Of course."

"I trust you too," chimed in Nara.

"Thank you. Stop doing everything for twenty-four hours," he'd held his hand up before she could object. "No housework, no studying, no reading or writing, nothing but watching TV and messing about with the kids. As soon as you're tempted to do something, repeat the quote and keep repeating it until you take notice."

He'd guessed she would break her promise, but she did manage sixteen and a half hours. That had been enough time for the message to sink in.

"Apparently, you questioned the good doctor, and going from the staff nurse's report, you spent an inordinate amount of time with Mrs Levy, to the detriment of the other patients. How do you plead?"

Tia felt about six inches tall. Here was the judge and she was up for the chop. She was one-hundred percent guilty as charged.

"Could you tell me what exactly happened, please?"

"The patient, Mr Berry, had told me that he had woken up in the night with a severe abdominal pain. When Dr Samuels stated that he was not going to give him any pain management, I thought I had to speak up."

"And you did. Several times by all accounts."

"But he didn't seem interested in what the patient was experiencing."

"And how about Mrs Levy?"

"Mrs Levy was a child refugee from Czechoslovakia and arrived in England alone during the war. No parents, friends or family, she only had her school satchel with her belongings in. I'm sorry, but when she started talking about her life, I became engrossed in her story and lost track of time."

"I see. First and foremost, I want to make it clear that this conversation of ours is confidential and is never to be repeated. Am I clear?"

"Very clear, Sister."

"Okay. To become a successful nurse, it is paramount that you should inform other professionals, including doctors, of any independent observations you may have. Furthermore, any discussions with the patient are essential in order for them to undertake a comprehensive assessment of the patient's current health. I would add that a good nurse always acts in a holistic person-centred way. This encompasses not only their medical but their social and psychological needs."

Nonplussed, Tia was still sitting on the edge of her seat. This conversation was beginning to feel more like an endorsement than a reprimand.

"In short, Tia, I am saying you have made an excellent start on our ward. However, you must remember that you work as part of a team. You are duty-bound to engage with your colleagues in a professional and cooperative way. You must learn to accommodate different points of view and recognise that diverse interventions have to be considered, not necessarily acted upon, but they must always be considered. Are you understanding what I am saying, Nurse Hearn?"

"I think I am, Sister," said Tia, taking a sip of water.

"Your penalty for these two events is simple. When you leave this office, you need to look sufficiently forlorn and suitably chastised. A career in the health service is one big balancing act. Talking of which, staff nurse Greenwich is a dedicated and experienced nurse. Whilst you're with us, you need to study her expertise and make the most of her professionalism."

Coming out of the office, she was aware that Greenwich was watching her. She walked straight to the nursing station to get her records up to date.

"Go for break, Tia," Greenwich said, coming up behind her.

Tia quietly left the ward, head bowed, aware that there was victory in her defeat.

CHAPTER 7
November 2019

Boris Johnson is now Prime Minister and calls a UK Election for December.

Donald Trump blames Californian Governor for Forest Fires.

The very first case of Coronavirus arises in China.

Jon

The last person Jon wanted to hear from was Ian fucking Tait. To hear from his daughters, even one of them, would have been great. To hear from his wife would be better than nothing. To hear from anyone in the world who wasn't Ian fucking Tait would have been more than welcomed.

"Jon Fox, how the devil is life treating you?"

"Sorry, who is this?" he asked, knowing full well who it was.

"Tait, Ian Tait."

"Ah, yes, from the University. How can I help you?"

"Just checking in to see how you are, old man."

Jon held the phone away from his ear. He could have thrown the phone across the room or simply hung up. Another choice was to repeat the advice he had given him the last time they had met. Natural curiosity forced him to make a fourth choice and to find out why this shrew of a man had contacted him.

"You keeping yourself busy?"

"Inundated with freelance work," Jon lied.

"In fact, I've got to go in five minutes. Due in Exeter this afternoon."

"Jolly good. I knew you would be alright. So, lecturing in Paddock's department? We worked together ten years ago. Say hi from me."

Piss.

"No, actually for the college there," he said, thinking on his feet. "Designing a new curriculum for them."

"Impressive. Well, I was wondering, if you have time, if you would front a project which has come our way. Unfortunately, we currently haven't the capacity to deliver but wondered whether you might. Although it sounds like you are far too busy."

"What is it?"

"A regional charity has asked us to organise and facilitate a conference for them."

"Name of the charity?"

"Mind Yourself."

"No need to be like that."

"No, that's the charity's name. Mind Yourself. It aims to help children and young people to maintain good mental health."

"Sounds fun," he joked. Tait still hadn't acquired a sense of humour.

"Do you fancy doing it?"

"How much money's in it?"

"Not a penny, I'm afraid. Your involvement would be out of the kindness of your heart. Has that put you off, Jon?"

"I'll think about it."

"There's only one thing, you have to decide soon, like in the next twenty-four hours. The original facilitator sent in his resignation from a Tibetan Buddhist Retreat in Scotland. The venue was already booked and confirmed, and the event publicised before it was fully organised. Some speaker slots are still unfilled." His voice was trailing off.

"When's it booked for?"

Tait told him the date.

"That's only four weeks' time."

Jon thought about his daily routine. Sleeping like it was going out of fashion. On a good day, out for coffee by eleven. Reading the Times or Guardian, end to end. A light lunch, maybe a bowl of cereal or soup or a hunk of cheese with bread, would be followed by the interminable curse of the afternoon—walking the river, driving out to Hengistbury Head or St Catherine's Hill. Once he, a religious atheist, had even attended a service in the priory. At six, the day came alive for a second time. Six o'clock was the time he gave himself permission to indulge in his first drink of alcohol.

"Send me the information. When I have a minute, I'll look it over."

"Splendid. Couldn't ask for more."

"I'm not promising anything."

Within a minute, his phone pinged; the email from Tait, complete with a twenty-page attachment. Having nothing else to do, he began reading the materials through.

Mind Yourself was run by young people for young people. Their stated aim was to promote resilient mental health and to empower young people to find their voices. On the back of a government grant, they were organising a conference in which people could share their stories and exchange coping strategies.

"Very noble," Jon said aloud, "but clearly not for me."

His phone pinged again as he waded through the good-meaning gunk. It was a message from Grace Carver of all people. The text said she was in the area on the way to an event she was facilitating. Would he like to meet for lunch? It was turning into a busy day.

What was it with Grace? He was at a loss as to her motives for staying in touch. He had apologised endlessly. He had told her he didn't want to see her again. He had even dared her to put the photographs out into the world. Who would really give a fuck? But she hadn't gone away. She hadn't sent the photographs anywhere. He knew it to be a lie, but perhaps she did fancy him after all. Of course, having a diary which was as blank as a field of snow, he agreed to see her.

Meeting up gave him the motivation to shower and shave. Not a bad thing. It also meant he had to forsake his joggers for a clean shirt and trousers. He arrived at the cafe fifteen minutes early and waited for her. Grace had suggested that she could pick him up, but he was ashamed of where he lived. He didn't want her to see how far he had fallen.

Every time he had seen Grace, she'd seemed taller, more self-assured and attractive. She carried a sense of self-possession which Jon found enviable. The tables had definitely been turned.

"Ending up in Christchurch is a great move. I think it's a lovely place."

"I haven't ended up anywhere. I'm in between things at the moment."

"And how is that going?"

"Perfectly. What do you think?"

"Maybe, you're struggling, maybe just a little bit?"

Without him being able to control it, Jon was becoming tearful. He pretended to cough in an attempt to divert her attention.

"Ah, I see it all now, Grace. You're really getting off on this, aren't you? The lechy lecturer bites the dust. You're enjoying all this, that's it, isn't it? I suppose you want me to say sorry again, you weirdo."

Grace took a deep breath and looked at Jon like a parent might look at a child who has yet again come into the house with muddy boots.

"Okay, Jon, I need you to learn a few facts. For a start, you don't have to say sorry. I knew you were sorry about a year ago. As for the photographs, I deleted them after I met you the very first time in that bar. And this you will find hard to believe; I actually do care about you. You know, I fell head over heels for you. In my naivety I was totally consumed by you. Oh, I knew you were a bastard even then but I still fell madly in love with you."

Involuntarily, Jon raised his eyebrows. "Don't worry," he said thoughtfully, "I was an immature child then. I was a right Boris Johnson. I was as shamelessly expedient without the hair or the power. Now ... Well, I'm not that anymore."

They must have sat in silence for five minutes, possibly more, as this information swirled around Jon's head. He could see himself lecturing in front of a crowded hall, he could see the innumerable students he had groomed for want of a better word. He could see the ending of his marriage, his arrival in Christchurch, the Weymouth Trip. Falling down in slow motion.

"You're a project manager, aren't you?"

"Wow! I wasn't expecting that."

"You fancy arranging a conference for young people's mental health?"

He shared with her a summary of the details, giving her the venue, dates and the provisional layout of the day.

"Why not?" she said. "There's only one thing …"

Lexi

Rayn's twenty-minute slot was scheduled for 11.40am. Already they were running ten minutes late. It had taken an immense amount of effort for her to agree to speak in the first place but this delay was only adding to her misery. Rayn, always brimming with confidence, was falling apart. When someone unhelpfully taunted her that she shouldn't concern herself, that there were only four hundred people waiting to hear what she had to say, she wondered if she would pass out.

Lexi was offering every platitude of reassurance she could think of. None were making the least impact.

"Breathe," she told her friend.

Rayn held Lexi's hand and took three long controlled breaths. In another world this may have worked but Rayn was intent on returning to her panic.

The last months had been a whirlwind for them both, but more so for Lexi. Sometimes a shadow of her old frailty would emerge without cause or provocation. She'd have to have a day, two at the most, away from the world, retreating to her bedroom. It had been her family who had worried most at these times. Lexi knew the difference between a lapse and a relapse. Her family though, had known no such thing and would hover about, fussing over her, asking if she wanted this or that. Despite herself, she'd taken to snapping at them, cutting them in two with an acidic phrase.

Lexi's phased reintroduction into school had been going well. It had felt like she was learning for the first time in her life. Her illness had wiped her mind clean, not in a negative way but in a way that rendered everything equally fascinating and mystifying. Through the illness, her powers of discernment had almost been completely obliterated. She hadn't wasted her time at home of course but returning to school, she'd been able to feel the benefits of discussion, debate and disagreement. Lexi had struggled with the fact that everything interested her. Every gem of learning sparkled. She'd been powerless to stop herself from pondering the meaning of whatever came her way.

Her teacher, Mrs Grenwood, had fed the addiction, dropping Lexi morsels of knowledge like an indulgent owner treating their dog.

Her parents had been worried that she was overdoing it. "Your poor old brain is going to explode."

Mrs Grenwood had countered this attitude to Lexi by quoting Leonardo Da Vinci: *learning can never exhaust the mind*.

In the spring, she had submitted her poem, *No Candles for Desert Places*, into a competition. It had failed to take any of the top prizes but was deemed to be highly commended. Much to her delight, she had been informed by her Great Aunt Ursula, who had been the organiser and one of the judges in the inaugural *Dorset Writing First* competition. Ursula had phoned her up, her dad handing over the house telephone with a mock solemn face.

"Don't think I had anything to do with your prize, Lexi. Nepotism would never do. All papers were anonymised when they went off to the judges. It was a friend who alerted me to your piece. He handed it to me and said: Wow! This is deep. And it was deep, Lexi, but also very beautiful. The line I loved above all others was: *and curiously, I spotted death and decided to follow her.* Absolutely loved it."

It had flashed through Lexi's head that if it was so brilliant, why didn't it rank higher, but she'd stopped herself being so deliberately ungracious.

"I think," Ursula had said, "no, I know you have been through a bit of an adventure of your own, Lexi. I can see it in your poetry. I think it's high time we met up, don't you? I haven't seen you since you could hardly speak, let alone write verse."

Then it had been Rayn's turn to come into the limelight. Out of the blue, she'd been contacted by a woman called Grace Carver. She had heard via a friend of a friend of a friend that she had experienced a devastating breakdown in her mental health and had started a very successful blog. Ten thousand regular followers was no small feat. Would she be willing to speak about her experience?

"No way," had been her immediate response.

Lexi had worked on her. "You simply must, Rayn! You think what you can tell others who get themselves in the same situation. You've got to do it."

Twenty-four hours later with Lexi directly behind her, Rayn had returned the call to Grace confirming that she would cover a slot.

The day had arrived and the two of them were behind the stage — one was protesting that she had nothing to say, the other one reminding her how brilliant her story was.

"You ready, Rayn?" Grace asked.

"No. I've decided not to do it, sorry and all that."

This was the third time Grace had had to cajole, bribe or insist that a participant should take to the stage and tell the audience their story.

"Wait here," said Grace. Rayn was hoping she was negotiating with another speaker to take her place but a minute later Grace appeared with an older man. "Rayn, let me introduce you to Jon Fox. Jon is a master of public speaking and he has a few tricks up his sleeve which may help."

"Hello, Rayn. Tell me what's going through your head."

"I'm shit. I don't know shit. What I have to say is shit. I haven't got a thing to tell those out there. They're going to have just one big laugh at my expense."

"Just think, all those people out there piss and crap the same as you. They're no better, no worse. They're just people."

"Is that your great contribution?" demanded Rayn. "Now I feel like I'm going out into one big latrine."

"Conceded. I have read your speech, Rayn, and I am not messing with you when I say I thought it was an amazing testament of someone who has been through hell and has come out the other end holding Freddie Kruger's hat."

The girls looked at each other, the reference going straight over their heads.

"How about if your friend here takes your place and reads it out on your behalf?"

It was Lexi's turn to shit herself. She was about to protest when, unknown to Rayn, Jon winked at her.

"Will you do that for your mate, Lexi?"

"I will." With that, Lexi grabbed the speech from Rayn's hand and marched towards the stage.

Rayn instantly recognised Jon's tactics. "Very clever, Jon Fox," and ran after her friend to snatch back her words.

Once out there, with a few laughs in, Rayn took over the floor. Her vivacity and honesty were uplifting, her natural humour compelling. At one point, she summoned a reluctant Lexi onto the stage and praised her friend's intuition and quick thinking for saving her life.

Rayn ran twenty minutes over and Grace had to come on to politely hook her off. A student nurse, Tia Hearn was next on and waiting in the wings.

"I think I got away with it," Rayn said to Grace as the applause was dying.

"Just about," she said.

Dexter

"We like you, Dexter, don't get us wrong, but you've been sleeping on the sofa for a week now. The children keep asking questions."

This had been his third sofa in the last six months. All had been pretty terrible and came to an unsatisfactory end. The first had been in a bedsit with his druggy friend, Brian. Dexter liked a smoke but for breakfast, dinner, tea and supper? So much lead to a permanent foggy head which stole the clarity he needed to do his work.

Sofa number two was even worse. Not only had Thirsty Kirsty been thirsty for a yard or two of real ale, but she had assumed that a man living under the same roof as a woman meant only one thing. He had been on her sofa but that hadn't stopped Kirsty eulogising the merits of a king size bed with a double-springed thirty-centimetre mattress.

She'd tried everything. She'd walked around the flat naked. She'd masturbated noisily. She'd burst into the bathroom when he was showering. Once he'd woken up to discover Thirsty Kirsty playing with his limp member. Eventually she'd succeeded; one night when he was falling apart, she'd offered him any fantasy he wished for. He'd known it was wrong and that Dee wouldn't see the funny side of it, should she ever find out. The fantasy involved a Dr Kirsty embarking on a thorough medical examination of Mr D. Jennings. She'd been investigating an unknown condition that made everywhere on his body ache until touched. It had been going as planned but his penis had had other ideas. Despite receiving an inordinate amount of attention compared to the rest of his body, its initial promise was replaced by a flaccid response. He'd left the next day.

Finally, to Deb and Pete's and their two children, Lily and Jay. As Christians, they couldn't let him be homeless. As Christians, they'd been duty-bound to remember their respective tattoos — the I-love-Jesus in a heart shape on Deb's arm and the huge empty cross which spanned Pete's back from top to bottom. And, as Christians, they'd had to set an example to others and tell their Christian colleagues of this small yet significant sacrifice they were making. However, after seven long days, Debs had wanted to kill him.

"I quite understand," Dexter replied, shoving his clothes into his holdall as Debs and Pete fumbled through various excuses. He had previously thought he was one of those Weymouth characters; a friend to all, a connector, a communicator, his shop the hub of a circle of relationships. Not so. Already he had run out of sofas and was wandering around town with a tatty holdall and a splitting black bag of clothes.

Dee had made it impossible for him. After the Lyme Regis incident, she had kept to her word. That first night, he had spent freezing to death in the car. When she'd opened the door after breakfast to find him standing on the doorstep shivering, she'd said, without malice or emotion, that she was surprised he was still there. His litany of pleases, sorrys and promises came to an end when she put her hand up as if stopping traffic.

"Dexter, I'm not talking to you. There is nothing you can do or say to change my mind. We will discuss what happens next when we get back home. In the meantime, the boys ..." she said, nodding towards the window where he spotted Andrew and Danny's little faces peeping through the blinds. "... the boys and I have planned our day out, and guess what. You're not part of it."

Dexter had followed them into Lyme but when Dee had seen him diving into a shop to avoid detection she'd made the point of talking to a policeman whilst pointing back to him. He'd hitchhiked back to Weymouth.

He'd been convinced that when they returned, Dee would see sense and allow him to stay in the house. He'd been willing to face conditions, make pledges and to generally assume a diminutive air for however long it took. The three days he'd been alone in the house were the longest ever. He'd kept pacing from room to room, talking to himself, watching disconnected fragments on television from any programme which happened to be on.

Dee hadn't responded to any of his texts or calls and neither had the boys. He hadn't dared contact anyone else as they all thought he was playing happy families on holiday in Lyme.

They'd been on their way home when Dee had texted Dexter: *We'll have our chat as promised, then I want you to leave the house.*

Receiving the message had triggered a new episode of pacing around the house, grappling with himself. He'd been sure she would relent and offer him a reprieve. Surely, it wasn't that serious. What had happened to his Dee, the Dee he had married, the easy-going Dee, the Dee who had always stood by him? Could there be some other factor that was influencing her? Her mother had never liked him. Her bitch friend Samantha had always been a jealous cow. Maybe—this could be it—she was having an affair herself and his misdemeanour was a mere excuse to bring matters to a head?

When the car had pulled up in the driveway, he hadn't been sure if he should rush out to them or stay put. Grabbing their bags and waddling to the front door, the family had appeared to be functioning quite happily without him. Dexter had opened the front door, greeting them with his wicked smile (never failed) rubbing his hands together and enthusiastically hopping from one foot to another. His efforts had been largely ignored. Under their mother's instructions, the boys had disappeared upstairs with their bags. Dee had slammed the boot shut and told him to go into the lounge.

"Four conditions."

"Only four!" he foolishly sang out.

"One, you're leaving the house now. Two, you can see the boys by mutual agreement, which includes their consent. Three, you will receive therapy for your fixation about conspiracy theories and all that nonsense. Four, you're not coming back until I give you the green light. That will only happen when I am one hundred percent convinced you have returned to the bloke I married fifteen years ago. Any questions?"

"None—I can do all that," he'd said, energetically.

"Notice I am not saying the marriage is over but imagine you are hanging over a cliff clinging on with one hand. The only thing which is stopping you falling is the tuft of grass you're holding. I hope you can feel your grasp slipping, Dexter. I hope you can feel the blades gradually starting to tear. In other words, if you mess up, its goodbye, farewell and fuck off."

As Christians, Debs and Pete had offered to give Dexter a lift to anywhere he wanted. Having nowhere to go, he declined and hit the streets with holdall and plastic sack.

His phone buzzed when he sat down on the sea wall. It was the Dorset-Anon group meeting in a local pub. Of course, the first Tuesday of the month. The world is on fire, went the headline, and we are the only ones who know the real reason why. At the very least, he could get wasted there and, you never know, a bed may follow.

Ursula

Greg Andrews was desperate to see Ursula. His message used the word urgent. Could she come to The Boot Inn for 1pm?

This was unfair, unacceptable and inappropriate. Already her day had been fraught with hiccups. She had forgotten to put the bins out and had to hurry downstairs in her nightgown, braving the ridicule of others. No sooner had she climbed the stairs when the doorbell rang. There was a parcel to sign for, a manuscript she had been asked to edit. The porridge exploded in the microwave and the bread became stuck in the toaster and smoked out the kitchen. It had been one of those mornings.

It was gone ten and the dogs were whining for their walk—and then this silly text from Greg. If it was urgent, why not phone her or, more sensibly, why not phone the police, ambulance, fire brigade or the coast guard whichever was most relevant?

The dogs were marched apace across the beach, puzzled by their owner's unusual briskness of speed and temperament. She curtailed the normal walk, telling her charges that if they wanted to blame someone, they should blame Mr Greg Andrews.

Back home, she realised she had been so consumed with indignation at the 'urgent' summons that she had actually forgotten to reply to him.

Regrets but I have an emergency of my own. She looked at it a couple of times and deleted it. *Love to meet up but today's hectic—Monday any good?* Ursula deleted that one too. With just over an hour to spare Ursula texted that 1pm would be fine.

The poetry competition had been a tremendous success. The Budmouth Writing Circle was on the map. The competition, with its special focus on encouraging young voices, had drawn the attention of newspapers, local and regional, and of the literary community.

The poet laureate had mentioned it in a speech as an example of how to generate enthusiasm for the next up-and-coming generation of poets. The fact that her great niece had won a highly commended slot was an added and unexpected bonus.

Ten new members had enrolled, two in their early twenties, and had helped the average age to slip below forty-five. And the newbies—as the 'oldies' referred to them — had wanted more debate, more criticism and more honesty. This hadn't suited some of the original members but it had suited Ursula's needs perfectly. She had always enjoyed stirring up perceptions and playing devil's advocate. Now she had a gang of others who would happily do this for her.

True to her word, Ursula had visited her nephew and family over the summer months. The drive down to Lyme she'd been dreading turned into quite a treat. She'd rarely travelled outside of the town. The MOT mechanic had accused her of winding the milometer backwards; nobody did less than 400 miles in an entire year.

She hadn't really known her nephew that well, let alone Lexi. Consciously overlooking the irritating mannerism he had inherited from her brother, she'd enjoyed the roast dinner she'd shared with them. The real highlight of the visit was walking to the end of the cobb with Lexi. Both had known they were kindred spirits the moment they'd met and the meal had been a necessary prelude before they were alone together.

"I had forgotten how beautiful it is around here. Bet you use this for inspiration?"

"Yes and no," Lexi had said. "I'm more interested in what happens to all this," a sweep of her arms across the bay, "when it enters this," she had said, tapping her forehead.

"Goodness me, how old are you again?"

"Sixteen."

"My head was cotton wool at that age. But we certainly share the same preoccupation now, Lexi, and that's what's important. As our dear friend Orwell says, reality exists in the human mind, and nowhere else."

"Exactly."

"Right, Greg. What is this so-called urgent matter?"

"Hello, Ursula. How are you today?"

"Don't you how-are-you-today me. I have rushed across town only to find you drinking lager and looking very un-urgent."

She realised she was being crusty and, seeing a red wine already on the table, she decided to pull her horns in and sit down.

"Now, what is it?"

He leaned into his briefcase and produced the first draft of her novel, *The Comfort of Blindness*. He poked it so forcibly, his lager spilt over.

"Ursula, this is sensational."

"I only gave it to you two days ago to glance over for any glaring errors and you're telling me you have read it cover to cover? Hard to believe."

"I read the last word of the ninety-seven thousand, two hundred and sixty-three words at four this morning. Once I started, I couldn't stop."

"Are you mad?"

"Only mad in praise of this." He gave the book another decisive poke. "It's brilliant."

This wasn't the reaction she had expected and she wasn't sure she liked it. Downing her wine in one, whilst watching Greg's unhealthy grinning, Ursula doubted whether she had made a sensible decision to allow him to read it.

"The lead up to Patrick's death was intoxicating, totally believable, almost relentless."

His death. Robert's death. Intoxicating? An absurd word to use. The reality had taken months.

Wishing that someone would keel over was foolhardy, let alone overwhelmingly malicious. If anything, the sheer desire to try and shorten his existence had seemed to lengthen it instead. Every day had been painfully long and fraught with the continual search for opportunity.

One such opportunity had arisen when she'd been reversing the car out. Robert had been sticking his nose in and unhelpfully guiding her out. Suddenly finding herself in a position of power at the control of nearly two tons of metal, an imbecile waving and shouting behind you, the temptation to press the accelerator fully down had been almost irresistible. Until, that is, their neighbour, Jessica Cragmore, had rushed into the view of her rear mirror as if willing to take his place.

She'd gone back to the stairs. On the top stair she'd busied herself unthreading the hem so that a lip appeared, one small enough to go unnoticed but large enough to catch the ungainly boot of an inebriated thug.

The weeks went by and Robert had remained as untouched as he was oblivious. She'd kept tweaking the 'crime' scene, moving the coat dresser closer to the bottom of the stairs, oiling the top stair with moisturiser. With every tweak she'd made, she had to make a conscious effort to remember, lest she be the victim and not him.

One night he'd clambered through the door at one in the morning. Struggling out of his coat, his huffing and cursing suggested that he had drunk the pub dry. She'd laid in bed listening, the dogs, having long ago given up greeting him, were equally attentive waiting for the accident to happen. She'd heard him piss like a horse and lumber into the hallway.

Please don't come in here. Please don't come in here.

Then the sound she had wanted to hear: a sickening yell as he'd thudded headlong down the stairs. The dogs had whimpered at the sudden noise, but they'd taken their cue from her and maintained their positions.

Silence.

Her heart had jumped into her throat. She hadn't wanted to check. She'd waited, breath heightened, wondering. A few minutes later she'd heard Robert come to with a groan. Her heart had sunk. He'd clumsily brought himself back to his feet, lumbered into the lounge and the next thing she heard was the overloud TV.

"Gadzooks!"

Ursula had hardly slept. By dawn, the TV still belting out, she had struggled out of bed and begun the long climb down the stairs, avoiding all the booby traps which laid in wait. She'd noted the splash of blood on the balustrade. The sight of his extended feet had infuriated her further. Followed by her canine apostles, she'd rushed to the kitchen drawer and taken out the knife with the longest blade. This was it. This really was it! She didn't care if they put her away for life. It would be worth it.

She'd marched into the lounge, the long blade ahead of her. Robert hadn't moved. He'd been sitting there, dried blood all over his face from a gash on his forehead. The man had already died. She'd studied him in amazement. When she spotted his boots untied, with loose laces, she'd chuckled. He had tripped over his own laces. The fall, the coroner had said, had obviously caused a bleed in the brain.

"This must be published, Ursula. It truly is a work of art. It must have been so difficult for you."

"How so?" she asked, defensively.

"I have heard your own husband was taken unexpectedly."

"It was difficult," she admitted, ordering a full bottle of wine. Au contraire, Mr Andrews, it had been the easiest story she had ever written.

Matthew

Although he was tempted to agree with Fiona this time, Matthew had signed up for The Fast for the World in two weeks. However, she was so adamant that he shouldn't join in, he stuck his heels in.

"The protests must continue! Fasting for forty-eight hours. That is four hours for each season of the twelve years before the tipping point."

"What tipping point?"

"When global temperatures will maximise and become irreversible. Don't you care about the future and the destitute world your grandchildren will inherit?"

Fiona prided herself on her ability to tolerate a raft of affronts or insults, however, a comment about her grandchildren proved to be the final straw.

"Shame on you, Matthew Price. Joy would be turning in her grave at your total stupidity."

"You have no right whatsoever to bring my late wife's name into the argument."

"You have no right to bring my grandchildren into it either. Since you've given up God you have been a self-righteous, sanctimonious chump."

"And you, Fiona Willis, have become a small-minded pernickety bore!"

At that, Fiona stood up, took off her apron and threw it into the corner of the kitchen.

"Is that how you feel?"

"That is exactly how I feel."

"Then I won't hold you up any longer. You won't be seeing the likes of me again. Have a good life—however many weeks that may be."

She left by the backdoor, slamming it shut with such force that a dish fell off the side and smashed on the floor.

Matthew was left at the kitchen table, nursing his cooling tea. He was merely being passionate. What was wrong with the woman? But with the sound of the door still ringing in his ears, he appreciated that he may have come across as cantankerous and pig-headed. But he was angry because he was right. Fiona had no right whatsoever to question his priorities. If he wanted to starve himself for a pathetic forty-eight hours to save planet earth, that's exactly what he would do.

He wanted to run after her. It annoyed him how much he depended on her. He couldn't operate without her. He took one absentminded bite of his cheese and pickle sandwich before, realising what he was doing, he threw it across the kitchen, landing on Fiona's discarded apron.

The best thing he had ever done was returning his dog collar back to the bishop. Since then, he had become alive once more. He was a volunteer for the food bank. He offered ad hoc counselling support for a local charity. He was an active member of the Extinction Rebellion and had super-glued his hand to the wall of the Bank of England. And, yes, had been arrested for civil disobedience. Granted he wasn't charged, but the six hours held in the police cell had been a highlight of his new godless humanitarianism. If he still believed in God, he would put his two fingers up and, like Abraham's Sarah, laugh in the old man's face.

He watched the early evening news and defiantly went to bed without a morsel passing his lips, a sort of preparation for the main event. Yes, he was making a demonstration of his commitment to a cause greater than himself. He was clearly exercising his willpower and suspending his tendency to call Fiona for his usual Thursday dish of shepherd's pie.

He wanted to fall off to sleep, allow the hours to pass in oblivion, and awake smug and triumphant, celebrating a full twenty hours without subsistence. But he couldn't sleep. This was dangerous. His usual pattern of falling asleep instantly was being tested. He recapped the argument with Fiona several times and every time came to the conclusion that she had been out of order. She had been downright rude and unnecessarily hostile. Contrary to her perception, since he had said farewell to God and all the hullabaloo which comes with him, his soul—for want of a better word—felt lighter and unburdened.

Lucy had been the final blow to his faith. He'd always felt his career had peaked too early anyway. Given the trajectory he had chosen at thirty, he may not have been a saint by now but he may possibly have become a bishop, or at least a rural dean.

Somewhere in middle age, he'd reached an invisible point when the sap of conviction had begun draining from him. Since Joy's accident he'd been able to almost physically feel the drip-drip-drip of his leaking self. The words of the services had become platitudes to a god who must have grown disillusioned and shot himself in the head with a celestial revolver centuries ago.

But it was Lucy who'd acted like a dam bursting its banks. It had been only a matter of time after Lucy went missing.

The police had phoned him directly and asked if he would be willing to support the family while they were waiting for news of their missing seven-year-old daughter. He hadn't hesitated and had been at the family's home within the hour. As soon as the door had opened, the mother, Suzy, had pulled him towards her and was already sobbing against his shoulder. When Suzy had released him, it was the turn of her mother, Patsy. The pain and the misery of the household had been tangible, the air unbreathable with grief.

The men of the household had wandered around the place distributing tea or beer, as silent and unfocused as shadows.

Lucy had been playing out with her friends in the street. It hadn't been late or getting dark. There hadn't been any traffic in the cul-de-sac where they'd lived. The ball games had been supplanted by hide and seek and that's when she'd gone missing. All the kids had thought she'd found the best hiding place but after half an hour of looking, one of the girls had knocked on Lucy's door to see if she had sneaked home.

For the next few days, Matthew had hardly left them. He'd offered comfort where he could, finding himself drifting from one anxious conversation to another. The mother in particular had wanted him to pray with her. Suzy had hardly let go of his hands while he'd asked Jesus to keep Lucy safe and bring her back to the family.

The police had called him first to help prepare him for the shock which was to come. Two officers would be arriving shortly to inform them that Lucy had been found. Her little body had been stuffed into a discarded length of cement piping.

When she'd been told the news, Suzy's screams had filled the house with unleashed rage Matthew had gone to hold her. She'd slapped him across the face, telling him to fuck off and take his fucking god with him. He'd understood of course, but her words had ripped into his heart like a litany for the lost and lonely. He'd shaken with humiliation.

Matthew was wide awake at nine in the evening, reliving these scenes for which there was no antidote. He could still feel the sting of the mother's hand. He could pretend or fool himself to some degree or balance it with reason but it was obvious that Lucy had become part of him.

He was starving by now, as well as terribly upset but was determined not to contact Fiona. He phoned Tia instead but she was not picking up. He followed it with a text: *Can you come over? Feeling so alone. Nothing to eat either.*

Half an hour later the doorbell rang.

Tia

"Are we mad or what?"

Helen Bond was driving Tia and Michelle to their first open water swim. Her new group of friends had worked on her. It wasn't her thing. Why would it be? She had been brought up on the coast and was a strong sea swimmer. Rivers never got a look-in.

This mixed group of nurses, one token doctor and a few other medical professionals, had discovered that they had two things in common: alcohol and swimming. At Michelle's thirtieth, there was much bragging about the merits of open river swimming. Many bottles of Prosecco later and the dare was agreed and accepted by all. Tia thought—hoped—it was the drink talking.

Tia had been reluctant to agree to any out-of-work plans. The logistics of living thirty plus miles away was a nightmare at the best of times. The children were her priority. Nara was in her last year of primary school already. Kojo would be starting school next September. Tia loathed shipping them around. On a day off, she would be sure to make a fuss of them. Organising an afternoon out by herself, an entire afternoon out, the children would always be something of a challenge. But her mum and Louise had both played their part in keeping the show on the road. Tia's sister, Kira, now fifteen, was increasingly proving to be a godsend.

To say that Tia was enjoying her nursing was an understatement. Unlike her colleagues, she'd never complained about the assignments. Quite the opposite, she'd cherished them and relished the demands it had put on her brain—like rain on the desert, she'd kept telling Louise. If Tia became too absorbed in a subject, Louise would indicate her growing boredom by popping in the question: is it like rain on the desert?

What had become clear was that Tia's previous interest in the human mind had not disappeared. If a choice became available, she would choose an assignment in which she could explore the psychological effects of illness.

An incident in Accident and Emergency had pushed her to make the decision to become dual-trained, qualifying in both mental and physical nursing care.

She shouldn't have been there at all, as her placement had been on a medical ward. They'd been short in A&E and Tia had volunteered. During her second day, a young man in his early twenties had suddenly run into the department shouting that the police were after him. He'd been convinced that they were out to kill him and he'd begged to be hidden. Everyone had been terrified and security had been called. The doctor Tia had been working with had told her to ignore him.

"Don't worry, it's mental health. Our psyche colleagues are abysmal at looking after their own."

Two security guards hadn't taken long to make matters worse by trying to grab hold of him.

"Guys, don't you understand, they are after me! I'm not making it up. They want my blood."

The guards hadn't listened. He'd started appealing to the other panic-stricken patients. One of the guards had raised his voice and told him that if he didn't leave, the police would be called. This had sent him into a paroxysm.

"You're signing my death warrant!" He broke free and deftly scuttled under a table and refused to come out.

The local mental health hospital had been contacted. Yes, they knew him, a chap called Pinar, and had been wondering where he had gone.

"We're sending round our staff. Could you make sure, you don't lose him."

It was the doctor's turn to burst into a frenzy. "We're trying to run an Accident department here, not a drop-in for lunatics."

Eventually, they'd persuaded David Pinar to come out from under the table and sit in an office for his own protection.

With a security guard on the door, Tia had been asked if she would sit with the patient until he was collected. Tia had felt very self-conscious but, clearing her throat, she'd asked David to tell her what was going on for him.

Coming from this petit student nurse, her quiet, unaffected voice had calmed him. He too had cleared his throat and told her what had been happening. By the time the nurses from the mental health hospital had arrived, David had been composed enough to leave unhandled and cooperative. The story he'd told was both fascinating and intriguing, this 'lunacy' was so interesting. It had brought to mind Jung's quote: *'Show me a sane man and I will cure him for you.'*

She'd inquired about dual-training shortly afterwards.

They were about eight strong when they gathered in the carpark at a lake outside Ringwood. Tia didn't know every one of them but the common excitement of plunging into the cold freshwater bound them together. Everyone was laughing or egging each other on.

The first footfall into the lake was followed by expletives and chortling. It seemed unbelievably cold, but the challenge was out there and they all tentatively hobbled in, their arms pathetically stretched out. Tia was wearing a pair of rubber shoes. Whether sea, river or lake, a slimy unseen bottom was not welcome. One chap roared and dived in, coming to the surface warning the others not to join him: it was so fucking freezing. It was enough to encourage the others.

One by one, they started throwing themselves in, timidly or otherwise, but always with a yelp or a scream. After a few minutes, Tia dived in and, finding that she was getting used to the temperature, she swam out further than the rest.

"Show off!" Helen shouted after her.

Tia dived under the surface and was amazed at the cool freshness on her body and the clarity of the water. She saw a shiny object on the bottom and decided to investigate. It was only a boring shopping trolley, but as she turned to resurface, the band of her shoe caught underneath one of the wheels. Pulling against it, only tightened its grip. The real struggle followed. She tried to dive to the trolley in order to prise it free but she was running out of breath. With all her strength, she was tugging away, lifting the trolley slightly, but not enough to release her. At that moment, one of the group appeared alongside her—a man she had seen around but not spoken to. He dived down and after a bit of fiddling about, tore off the shoe and set her free.

She tried to reassure them that she was alright. She was fine, she insisted. There was nothing to worry about. She had been stupid. It turned out that the man who had rescued her was Henry Banks, a radiographer based at a sister hospital. Various jokes were made about him having x-ray vision and that he could see right through her. But he was gracious when she thanked him and shook his hand formally.

"Just one thing," she said, "you owe me a new pair of shoes."

Helen drove her home. As they were approaching town, Tia's phone flashed a message from Matthew: *Can you come over? Feeling so alone. Nothing to eat either.*

She persuaded Kira to stay for another hour when she threw financial caution to the wind and taxied over to Portland, a frozen meal she had taken from the freezer balanced on her knees. When she was getting out of the car, she was surprised to bump into Fiona also carrying a meal.

"I think we've been played," Fiona said. She told Tia how obnoxious Matthew had been earlier in the day. "I can't believe his ingratitude but as you see, I have relented. Not before he contacted you though."

Tia showed her his text.

"Ah, poor little old man!" At that, both of them burst into laughter, the laughter quickly turning into hysteria. Fiona had to set the meal down on the wall and steady herself on the gate.

"And I almost drowned today," Tia said, which set them off on another spree of laughter.

They were still at it when Matthew appeared at the door in his pyjamas, buttoned up the wrong way. He couldn't see what was so funny, these two women laughing their heads off. Each was holding a plate of food as if they had crossed the line in some absurd meal-on-a-plate race.

Matthew had rehearsed a pathetic tearfulness but soon he was joining in with a joke that had no origin, hadn't even been told, had no meaning whatsoever, but somehow it turned out to be the funniest joke in the world.

CHAPTER 8
March 2020

The UK ceases to be an EU member following the Conservative landside win with the slogan 'Get Brexit Done'.
Labour suffer the worst defeat since 1935.

Coronavirus is a global pandemic with many countries, including the UK, opting for national lockdowns.

Trump downplays the threat from the virus as a temporary nuisance.

Jon

"For fuck's sake," said Jon, making the mistake of turning on the news. "Two minutes ago he was saying we could wash our hands for twenty seconds and all will be well, and now it's going to be a lockdown. Total and complete, everything coming to a halt. Including me."

After the conference, he had been asked to arrange a follow-up event on focusing on the influence of social media on young people. He knew very little about social media and not much more about the youth of today, but the apparent success of the Mind Yourself event had attracted wide and unexpected attention.

In truth, Grace had been the driving force behind the last one. She was familiar with the complexity of logistics and the need for a measured and orderly approach; skills Jon struggled with. His flare was to see the conference in broad terms, widening its remit and selling it to others as a viable project.

They had chosen the speakers well. Collectively they had been a broad, robust representation of young people who were awake to the dilemmas in modern life. The natural way it had fallen into place fitted in with his laissez-faire style. Someone knew someone, who knew someone, who knew someone. A neighbour, for example, a member of the Budmouth Writing Circle who had heard about the conference, knew a woman, Ursula Bird, from the same group who had a great niece who'd done well in a poetry competition, who had a best friend who'd attempted suicide.

The only person Jon had approached directly was Tia Hearn. After Ben, his ex-landlord's son, had taken him to Weymouth on that terrible trip, he'd seen her discarded mail and heard her being described by Ben as a real treat. The nature of her experience had played on his mind and he'd kept wondering what had happened to her. Synchronicity came into play.

The university, being as inefficient as ever, had neglected to take him off their generic email distribution. To rub salt into his wounds, they had revamped his course—his course—as Critical Theory for Professions in the Caring Sector. He had thought at the time that he would lodge an official complaint. He had always thought of himself as a victim of constructive dismissal and this repackaging of a similar if not identical course was evidence to that effect. But despite possible financial recompense if he won, he couldn't be arsed. He couldn't be bothered to contact the bastards, let alone make a fuss and put together a case. He had turned his back on Tait et al and didn't give a flying fuck about critical thinking or the university.

However, he was copied into a list of potential students for the revised course. He had been about to delete it when he'd seen Tia's name. Was this the same Tia Hearn? It must be, surely? How many Tia Hearns could there be living in the South of England? If it was indeed the very same, how did the real treat end up on a nursing course?

Using his university email address, he had messaged her. He'd informed her that he was arranging a conference for Mind Yourself and wondered if she was interested in contributing to the programme. He'd attached the information pamphlets with the purpose, remit and intended outcomes. To give it some credibility, he'd signed him off as a university lecturer — retired.

He'd heard nothing for a week and had resigned himself to locating someone else to undertake the pre-lunch slot. An email had arrived from her, confirming his intuition. Most certainly, it read, I can talk about the effects of abuse on mental health. Her contribution on the day had been breathtaking, making connections between trauma, the mind's response and the consequences on one's health.

He had stayed in touch and had been considering whether she may be useful for any future event or initiative but with all this lockdown business, he wondered whether any follow-up to the conference would ever take place. Surely this nonsense about the virus would be over soon enough?

He was percolating his second cup of coffee when Grace phoned, confirming his concern.

"Any guesses why I'm phoning? Every project I am working on has been suspended until further notice. I think it highly unlikely that the Social Media event is going to happen."

"It wouldn't be until the summer."

"The word on the street is that the lockdown is going to last at least until June. I think we will be hearing from our sponsors by the end of the week. It won't be good news."

Jon was surprised at how profoundly the call affected him. When he needed to think, Jon had got into the habit of walking around the priory grounds. Of all things—he had been on the brink of reinventing himself, of moving away from his old tattered identity. The last couple of years had remorselessly poked and jabbed at his sense of self. The conference had been a vindication of sorts that he wasn't a complete jerk.

The Weymouth fiasco had propelled him to quit the studio flat as quickly as he could. He'd ended up paying his way out and left after ten weeks. His landlord had got away with three months' worth of free money. As a poor consolation, Jon had written directly to the landlord informing him of his son's abhorrent behaviour towards vulnerable women and, to reinforce the message and give it a bit of clout, he had copied in the local police department.

  Waiting for a divorce, the matrimonial monies were beginning to be sorted, enabling Jon to shift into a rented two-bedroom house nearer to the town centre. It was a modern build with boxy, functional rooms but it was much better than the studio flat. From one bedroom window, he enjoyed a framed view of the river.

By the time he'd walked around the priory a couple of times, he was calm again. Lockdown in 2020? What did that even mean? The plague in the Twenty-first century? But, he couldn't change a thing. Creating a fuss—kicking off, lamenting that the world wasn't doing what he wanted—was a fundamental waste of time and energy. There was nothing he could do about it other than to accept it.

Walking around the corner to his house, he saw a young woman sitting on his doorstep, smoking a cigarette, looking at her phone. It wasn't until he was nearer that he realised it was his eldest daughter.

"About time," she said, standing up.

"What in the hell are you doing here, Victoria?"

"Waiting for you."

"I can see that, but why?"

"In a nutshell, I have fallen out with prickface and couldn't abide living with him in lockdown. I thought I would come to live with you."

"Who's prickface?"

"My ex, James. Get a grip, Dad, I have been going out with him for virtually a year."

"Well, I'm sorry, Victoria. You can't live here."

"Uh, why?"

"I'm not sure yet. I'm still working out my reasons."

"A. Are you my father? B. Have you a spare room? C. Do I need somewhere to live during lockdown? It's yes to every one of those questions, Father. I am moving in."

"You would be much better off with your mother and little Sophie."

"You're forgetting her lover boy. He makes prickface look like a nice guy. No, I've made up my mind. It's you or the streets."

There were several practical reasons why he didn't want Vicky to live with him and a few more familial reasons. Yet, she moved in anyway. He had to order a second bed that day but Vicky didn't care about that. She took his room until it arrived.

"You don't mind, do you, Dad?" she asked him, already changing the sheets.

"Let's pub it" she said at five in the afternoon.

"Do you realise we are in the middle of a global pandemic and keeping away from other people is considered wise?"

"A. Are we going into lockdown? B. Is this one of the last times we can drink in a pub? C. Are you gasping for a drink as much as I am?"

"Please stop A-ing, B-ing and C-ing me!"

They even enjoyed a lock-in before lockdown, drinking shots until one in the morning. When Jon came to the following day, he felt like he had been run over by a bus. For a split second, he wondered why he was sleeping on his sofa. Through a fuzzy head, he recalled the chaos of the previous evening. And then, with a sudden pinch of reality, he remembered that upstairs, in his bedroom, in his bed, his daughter was sound asleep.

Lexi

No, no, no! It was a big no from Lexi Morgan. Lockdown could not and would not happen.

Who had ever heard of such a notion? Forced self-isolation, as if they were somehow trapped in a Kafkaesque world—all guilty of an unknown crime. In the final days of school she became increasingly defensive, at home increasingly quarrelsome.

"It's injustice on a global scale," she complained to Rayn. "Only the malicious God of the Old Testament could conjure this one up."

Rayn told her to get a grip. She understood all too well why Lexi was reacting in the way she was. Unlike anyone else she knew of, Lexi had already experienced a lockdown of her very own.

Lockdown filled her with dread. Lexi was worried that the stranger who'd sought her out all those years ago had now been externalised, had grown grotesque, monstrous, and was even more destructive. Her memory filled with the endless days, minimal contact from anyone outside her family, only able to watch the world live on, bravely and vivaciously while she was chained to her bed.

The dreaded feeling of being continually caught in a time loop haunted her—waiting for a train which had already left the station. Now this. Now the world retaliating and imposing a vicious suffocation. Her beloved schooling would cease, going out with friends would cease, seeing Rick, her new boyfriend, would cease.

"I'm not having it, Rayn."

"What you going to do then? Write a strongly worded email to the prime minister?"

Mrs Grenwood tried to reassure Lexi that her studies would continue. The assignments were as before, and the recommended books would remain the same. What would be different would be the discussion or lack of it.

"You have to think," Mrs Grenwood told her, "we have mobiles which never leave our sides. We have Zoom. We have our online chat room and virtual libraries. In the last pandemic, a hundred years ago, only the rich and famous had phones."

Rayn reminded Lexi that the blog was online. That would continue—she joked with Lexi that her computer was one hundred percent virus-free.

Ursula, who she was in regular contact with now, wrote to her to say that reality is best preserved through poetry. If you don't like what's happening, write about it.

She had chosen to ignore Rick for months. When he had called Plath's poem cool, she'd been instantly aware that he was interested in her. With a secret resolution, she'd taken little notice of his notes and the appearance of a solitary kiss after his name. Lexi had taken his nods and stares in a good-humoured way, determined not to read too much into them.

She hadn't been able to avoid admitting to herself that the bottom line beneath her aloofness was simply that she was embarrassed. All her missed schooling and the deficit of peer interaction had led to a coyness which verged on immaturity. Other than Jacob's awkward touching of her breast, she hadn't had any real experience of expressing her sexuality.

One night she had shared the bed with Rayn and had felt a tension sourced in the newness of lying against another, but nothing had come of it. Rayn, she'd known, had lost her virginity in Lyme Woods to Kevin Redford. Rayn had liked to joke she'd lost it twice; the second time to Josh Roder, the only one which mattered.

She and Rick had kissed; kissing had become snogging, or, as Rayn had jokingly called it, sucking face. But they had reached a point where both were at a loss as to where they should go next. Rayn had helped, or not helped with the rhyme:

Lips and neck
Followed by any limb
One tit, then two
And finally, your quim

Now it was lockdown, it would be impossible to capitalise on the first line, let alone progress to the second.

The family discussion on whether Lexi should be shielding resulted in a shouting match, which, except for Harry who was oblivious to what was going on, ended with the whole family in tears. Lexi threw her dinner at the wall. Her parents had to settle for adopting a cautious approach, mindful of her susceptibility.

"We're going to stick rigidly to the rule book," declared her dad, in an attempt to assert himself. "We have to keep our family safe and safe means keeping ourselves to ourselves. We will uphold the law of the land."

Rayn facetimed Lexi first thing on the first day—for her, this meant before ten in the morning.

"I have read through all the government's bumf and have found a few get-out-of-jail cards."

"Dad said there was no such thing."

"But there are three of them. Exercise allowed once a day. Food shopping allowed as and when necessary. And if you are a volunteer, supporting a vulnerable person."

"But we're not allowed to meet up in pairs."

"But, little Miss Stickler, there's nothing stopping us accidentally on purpose bumping into each other, is there?"

Suddenly, Lexi was jogging. She had never jogged in her life; her parents were very wary and because she remained a little wobbly on her feet, advised against it. That, of course, only made her more single-minded.

"You would rather I was morbidly obese after lockdown?"

The jog was more like a walk with attitude. She ran the same route in a loop at the edge of the woods and, low and behold, she would bump into Rayn in her purple joggers. Conveniently, they would both need a break at the same time. Out would come the pre-rolled cigarette and a single match. Sometimes, as part of their fitness regime, Rayn bought a small flask of gin and tonic.

Carla joined them a couple of times.

Molly said that she would rather get the plague than jog anywhere.

Volunteering to help the elderly became their number two activity. They both turned up on the doorstep of an unsuspecting neighbour to undertake any essential shopping. Nobody was sure if they could do this as a twosome. Lexi's dad contacted the police but they weren't sure either. Lexi and Rayn made noises about social distancing and the use of masks as a way of maintaining their safety. They made a case that this was their civic duty in a time of crisis and any concerns about safety were forgotten in favour of the greater good.

All was going well when she received a card with a heart on from Rick. It read like the plea of a dying man: *Lexi, I must, must, must see you! Can't wait. Don't want text or facetime, need to see you in person. Real urgent. Rick.*

The note was followed by a page of kisses.

"I recognise that tone anywhere. He wants a screw," Rayn affirmed.

"Don't be silly, he wants nothing of the sort. Anyway, no can do, vis-a-vis Mr Coronavirus, aka Covid-19"

"I believe he's thinking more Coitus-69."

Dexter

"How comes it's you? Where's Barbara?" Dexter asked.

"I'm sorry but I'm the fill-in for the fill-in. Barbara's sick with this virus and so is her substitute Mary, so you have ended up with me. And that's only just. I think with the coming lockdown next week, face to face contact won't be allowed. We'll have to do it all on zoom, whatever that is."

"You're the priest, aren't you?" Dexter asked.

"Who told you that?"

"That's what they all call you."

"Well, I have told them again and again, I am no longer a priest and haven't been for a number of years now."

"What's that mean then? Did they kick you out for something dodgy?"

"Ha! I guess you would say I lost my faith. But we are here for you, not me. I read Barbara's notes, so I know a little about you."

"What did she write about me? That I've fucked up and I'm only here because I want to get back home to my family?"

"Nothing of the sort," Matthew said, attempting to be light.

"She said you were struggling with your beliefs."

"Shows how much she's been listening. I don't have beliefs, I have facts I live by."

"But," said Matthew, trying not to get riled, reminding himself it had been some years since he last counselled anyone. "But these facts have seemingly left you at odds with your family. That's another fact." Matthew could tell Dexter was trying to work out if he was poking fun at him or not. "Tell me where you think you are," he continued. "Is this counselling helping, do you think?"

Dexter was adamant that he wouldn't divulge what had happened in the previous week. Not that anything had actually happened. Any reminder or indication of what was buzzing through his head would be catastrophic in terms of getting back with Dee. Dexter was now sleeping in a cupboard he'd cleared out in the shop. It was the last option.

As the time away from the family home became longer, he'd realised he needed a more satisfactory solution than the hazardous existence of sleeping on other people's sofas. He'd cleared the cupboard out of all his old equipment; the vacuum cleaner, brushes and cleaning stuff were forced into the tiny attic space or jammed behind a Japanese screen. He'd found out that there was about enough room for a basic pump-up bed and a sleeping bag; his feet stuck out of the door but otherwise it was adequate.

Technically, he wasn't allowed to sleep in the shop. It was one of the contractual clauses which could result in termination but with the world going mad, he'd calculated that this little misdemeanour would pass unnoticed. Washing in a sink which was about the same size as a fruit bowl was problematic to say the least but he managed. Nobody could call him out on his personal hygiene.

Coronavirus and the possibility of vaccinations had invigorated the group with new purpose. To the absolute fact that the virus was part of a premeditated plan or the consequence of government action, there was not one dissenting voice; the disagreements had come as to which was most likely.

Some had favoured that the cause was the installation of 5G aerials for the latest batch of new mobile technology. Nigel Glover had blamed Bill

Gates—but he blamed Bill Gates for everything. The consensus had been that the Freemasons and the Illuminati had combined to cut unwanted populations down. No surprise, the poor were dropping like flies, not to mention black, Bangladeshi, Chinese and Indian people. And obese people, bawled out Tony, who had a BMI of forty. Bastards.

As for vaccinations, should they come along, the group had long established that these would change your DNA or contain Mercury or would be used to inject detection devices into your blood stream. Some had been of the opinion that all three were true.

"Whose children have been vaccinated?" asked Ki Hbj—pronounced Kee Jay; the h and b were silent—who had changed her name from Sheila Robertson. Some of them may have been lying because only Dexter and Georgia had put their hands up. 'Watch them,' had been Ki Hbj's advice.

"But I had all the jabs as a kid," Dexter had protested.

"So did I," Ki Hbj had said, "but the mercury wasn't introduced until 2000, so we are all in the clear."

"Why 2000?"

"The Millennial bug," Ki Hbj had retorted, rolling her eyes as if explaining it to a child. The rest had readily assented. "There's another story," she'd added.

Nigel had thought about mentioning Bill Gates but decided to keep it to himself.

"What does that mean?" Dexter had dared to ask another question. "For the kids, I mean?"

"Just watch them, I would advise," she said, not for the first time. "Eventually, maybe not today, maybe not tomorrow but one day you are going to find that their loyalties may lie elsewhere and not with you."

It had been Dexter's time for the children. The routine for having the boys had become fixed relatively quickly after the split, or, the trial separation as Dexter preferred to call it. He had them Sundays, as the shop was closed, and Wednesday evenings.

On that particular Wednesday, he'd decided to drive out to Durdle Door. The boys had grown used to these little trips exploring the county, which would have remained undiscovered if their parents had still been together. The boys had also realised that with the separation came additional treats; both mother and father provided treat meals and unexpected gifts. Neither Andrew nor Danny had wanted the separation but as it had happened, nobody could blame them for capitalising on it. After Durdle Door, for example, it would be Kentucky Fried Chicken.

The incident Dexter had been adamant on keeping out of his conversation with Matthew had occurred when the three of them stood on the cliff looking down onto the stone arch and watching the sun go down.

"How is it living without your dad in the house?" he'd asked them.

The boys had known such questions were emotional traps, which both Dee and Dexter used shamelessly on their children. They had muttered that it was okay.

"But you must miss me?"

"We do, Dad," braved Andrew, "but we have got used to it."

"But," Dexter had continued, "It's not the same?"

"Yep, it sure is different," Danny had said. The way he'd blurted it out had sent the boys into a giggle, the giggle turning into hysterics. Dexter, not party to the joke, had looked at his boys keeling over and one thought had come to his mind: vaccination.

When they'd got back in the car, the boys had still been chuckling away. They'd parked on the hill overlooking the sea. Fleetingly Dexter had thought how easy it would be to let the handbrake off, to throw himself out of the moving vehicle and let them plunder down the hill, leaping over the cliff and smashing onto the beach below. He'd discovered that already his shaking hand had been clutching the handbrake. One simple movement and the car would begin to roll, the boys' wicked laughter would change to screams and that fucking smile Dee was always smiling would be wiped off her stupid face forever

"Shut the fuck up!" he'd ended up screaming at the boys. They'd immediately fallen silent.

Matthew knew he was getting nowhere with Dexter. He knew that he should be non-judgemental and impartial in his approach but he was struggling with him. The combination of arrogance and ignorance was the worst of all combinations.

"You must know what it's like," Dexter was saying. "You had religion and I bet you got annoyed when you came across people who thought it was just a load of crap."

"Not really. I accepted that my beliefs weren't everyone's cup of tea."

"But you were certain you were right?"

"At one point I was. Then I realised that they were my beliefs. They weren't facts."

"That's where we differ."

"Beliefs are an acceptance that something exists or is true, but fundamentally they come without proof."

"I have proof."

"You have belief. I came across a quote by a philosopher called Nagel. He said that he didn't believe in God and he didn't want the universe to be like that. That's what I thought: I don't want to live in a world where God exists. So, I changed my belief. Apply this to yourself, Dexter. Do you really want to live in a world where your beliefs are actually true? Drop the belief and you're free again — to go back to your family and enjoy an ordinary life."

"I can see why they chucked you out," Dexter said getting up from his chair.

"Keep safe," replied Matthew.

"Oh, don't worry about me. The virus is only interested in misbelievers."

The following day, both Matthew and Dexter experienced symptoms of Coronavirus. Whether Matthew infected Dexter, or the other way round, or they had contracted it separately elsewhere, no one would ever know.

Ursula

She could hardly believe it. On her kitchen table was the complete edited version of her novel *The Comfort of Blindness*. If she was to read through it one more time, she had said to Greg, she needed to print it out.

The computer was such a convenience but nothing could replace its digital detachment more than the physicality of hard copy. And there it was — the story actually existed and the only person she had told, other than Greg, was Lexi.

When Lexi had heard she'd written a story, she'd practically begged Ursula to send her a copy. They were in frequent contact now, agreeing to write to each other, not using email or text, but choosing to write in longhand — with a pen on actual paper, placed in an envelope and mailed with a stamp on it.

Ursula had a great deal to be grateful for with regards to Greg. His enthusiasm for her story had led him to contact a friend whose sister was an agent. He'd pressed Molly Keen to read it as a top priority. Not used to being pushed or commanded to do anything, the agent had picked up on Greg's passion and conceded. The sole problem was that he'd neglected to tell Ursula.

The following Monday, Molly had telephoned her directly. Ursula had assumed it was a scam and promised to inform the police. When Molly had persevered, Ursula had finished the call by telling her to piss off and had slammed the phone down with a sense of justified outrage. She'd visibly strutted around the kitchen, proud of her abrupt and decisive action. But the look Desmond had levelled at her had given her a moment of doubt. She'd phoned Greg, who'd sheepishly confirmed to her that he had sent it.

"You would have just sat on it, Ursula." She'd told him to give the draft back to her and to never darken her door again.

Another triumphant, self-righteous lap around the kitchen. How dare he? It amounted to stealing or fraud or false representation—she hadn't been able to put her finger on the exact nature of his crime but she'd been positive he was guilty of one. She'd done everything to avoid Desmond's gaze but when her eyes had fallen on her loyal mutt he'd been looking at her in a questioning way.

Before she'd decided she would erase his contact details and block him on all forms of communication, her phone pinged. She'd read the text anyway: *the next call you get will be from Molly Keen. If you have nothing to do with me again, that's up to you but please take her call.*

She'd taken the call. Molly Keen had apologised for calling her out of the blue. She had read *The Comfort of Blindness* in three sittings. Molly had praised its vitality and its vivaciousness.

"I loved the use of the present tense," she'd continued. "It seemed like it really happened, reading less like fiction and more like the truth."

Ursula had almost wanted to counter it with "actually, it's a truth which reads like a fiction," but she'd held her tongue.

Molly had confirmed that reading in three sittings had only happened twice in her twelve years as an agent. When she'd told Ursula the name of the other writer, Ursula had shaken her head in disbelief.

"I will have no problem finding an editor and then a publisher. In short, Miss Bird, would you do me the honour of accepting me as your literary agent?"

She'd made Greg suffer for a day or two; any longer would have been cruel. He'd had to wait to be rewarded for his efforts. Not until the process of contracts and edits had begun had she taken him out for an Italian dinner to thank him for his trouble.

There it sat on the kitchen table, all four hundred and twenty pages of it. She had been worrying whether the story amounted to a true-life dot-to-dot picture of everything which happened. Would the police be interested in what was effectively a confession? Would the coroner reopen the case?

She'd concluded that nobody would be interested enough in the death of a loser; nobody cared enough about the twat to raise any questions over his demise. In the end, she was in her fifties and would let the world decide. Until then, she'd emphasise that it was just a story. Yes, she'd drawn on a troubled relationship with her former husband, but essentially it was a tale she wanted to tell.

Greg came around that evening, ostensibly to see how the edit was going. Knowing that Ursula was so absorbed in the rewrite, she would have forgotten to eat; he arrived with an armful of fish and chips and a bottle of red wine. These gifts, he hoped, would soften the request he had in mind.

The news was buzzing with the advance of the Coronavirus and the resultant national lockdown.

"It will mean that we can't see each other," Ursula said. "Maybe it is just as well. I've got all this work going on. I hadn't realised editing would be so bloody difficult and time consuming."

"You've done it before though, haven't you?"

"Yes, but this is for real. I'm quickly discovering that the publishing business is ruthless. Writing it was easy compared to this."

"There is another way to approach this," Greg suggested.

"Any tips are more than welcome."

"I don't mean the editing. I mean us."

"Sorry, Greg, you're losing me. What us?"

"Think on it. This lockdown could go on for months. At the moment, I see you almost every day. Lockdown means lockdown, no contact or bumping into you or meals or drinks or conversations — well, none in person."

"I suppose that is the way it is."

"But that's what I'm saying. It doesn't have to be."

A silence grew between them as Ursula struggled to understand what Greg was getting at.

"Am I being thick here?"

"I am sorry to say, Ursula, for all your massive intellect, you are being thick."

Then the penny dropped. "Out of the question," she said, knocking back her wine. "Are you seriously suggesting, Gregory Andrews, that you move into this house, my house, over lockdown?"

"That, Ursula Bird, is exactly what I am suggesting."

"But as what? A friend?"

"Friend or something more ... friendly."

Without answering, she got up and began clearing the plates away. She disappeared into the kitchen. He could hear her talking to the dogs and letting them out into the yard. When she returned to the lounge. it was as if she was startled to see that Greg was still there sipping his wine.

"Greg, I'm suddenly feeling quite tuckered out, would you mind if we call it a night?"

He was out in the cold night air within minutes, feeling foolish and irritated with himself. He had messed up, big time.

Ursula had a rough night, up and down to the toilet, a cough waking her up, the pets as unsettled as she was. In the morning, she made some tea and toast as usual and sat in front of the television, absorbing the endless drawl of politicians and medics, all concerned with the spread of the virus and the rise in the death rate. The lockdown was definite and would start on Wednesday 23rd March.

As she drank her tea and she ate her toast, it dawned on her that she hadn't tasted anything. She lit a joss stick and couldn't smell it. Bloody hell, bloody hell, bloody hell!

"Greg, I have the plague." She listed her symptoms, punctuating each with a dry cough. "It's definite. I probably gave it to you too, you know."

"Shall I come around?"

"Yes, I would like that," she said. "Maybe bring some overnight things with you."

Matthew

It wasn't the rasping cough or his struggling lungs which were getting on his nerves. It was simply the social isolation.

He'd had another run-in with Fiona. It wasn't as dramatic as the last time; he'd made a concerted effort to pull back before it got out of hand. The whole episode had served to remind him that he relied on her, more so now he was unwell.

"Self-isolation means self-isolation," Fiona had told him.

"Aha! But I am allowed out for exercise!" he'd chirped back at her.

"Not if you actually have the virus. It's staying at home with no exceptions unless you get worse and have to go into hospital. If you want to exercise, do push-ups in your garden."

"But you're allowed in because you are part of my support bubble."

"Matthew, we have been through this. It's got to be for direct care only and then I would have to put my armour on before I could go anywhere near the likes of you."

He had to admit defeat and accept that he was home alone, maybe for some time. Fiona did most of his shopping and provided a hot meal once a day. The daily delivery was set on his doorstep with a knock on the door and a quick chat over the garden gate.

Occasionally, Tia came over to the island, but now with this virus she, as a student nurse, had to be doubly cautious and had even less time to spare.

After this little daily interaction, he was left to stew in his own juices. He thought he would go insane. He made it a rule not to switch the television on until seven in the evening. This was quickly revised to five o' clock and anytime on the weekends. He made pointless phone calls about his pension or to the council on anything from local planning or rubbish collection. He got used to being on hold. He phoned the talking clock twice.

Appearing like magic through his letterbox, a package of medication was delivered by the local surgery every two weeks. Fiona had to contact his doctor because she was worried about Matthew's wheezing. Dr Michaels interviewed him through the window. He increased the frequency and the strength of his respiratory medication and added a low dose of diazepam.

"Do you think I'm crazy then?"

"Not at all. Take one if you become panicky or over-anxious especially if you are struggling to breathe. It will calm you down nicely."

A few weeks into the period of isolation, Matthew metaphorically slapped himself across the face and began the process of embracing his fate. Stepping down from resistance mode to confinement allowed him the time to relax and adjust.

He had basically been sulking. Part of this defiance, he came to realise, was not only the enforced imprisonment but his growing awareness of his age and his vulnerability. He was going to die sooner or later. Naturally, he had always known that but the wheezing was a constant reminder that he was nearer to death than he would have liked. He was feeling better and with a little help from the diazepam, his sleep was wonderfully deep, but the ultimate question remained: how much sand was there left in the hourglass?

His faith had provided a blanket of comfort; without it he was truly alone. To his own annoyance, he still harboured notions of Joy waiting for him when his time was up but these amounted to ideas designed for consolation and protection against melancholy. He decided on a massive overhaul.

This proved wonderfully time-consuming and much more entertaining than he could have imagined. Bonfires became an exciting daily experience. He couldn't believe all the utter crap he had accumulated over the decades. There were files of letters, fuel bills, fifty years of car MOTs, lapsed insurance policies, hymn sheets, funeral itineraries, notes, lists and birthday cards. A bank statement from 1969 was the epitome of his lifetime of hoarding.

The ritual blazes were hypnotically cathartic. His neighbours weren't so passionate about them. When the wind came from the north east, Ernie said his house smelt like it was on fire. Matthew tried to persuade him of the importance of what he was doing but agreed to check the wind direction before lighting up.

Taking it carefully, he managed to climb up into the attic. He knew Fiona would have hit the roof if she had known, but who was going to tell her? So far, the burnings had been limited to impersonal and formal stuff. Up in the attic, there were boxes of the substance of his life. After hours of rumination, he decided to destroy his box of sermons. Who would read them now? And, should he die tonight, all he was doing was saving Fiona the trouble.

Peeling the patch of sermons off one by one turned out to be harder than he thought. Catching odd phrases and sentences, some of which he could recall writing, rendered him tearful and reflective. Interestingly, he came upon one entitled God is Dead. It was an analysis and rebuff to Nietzsche's stance. And when he placed the last sermon into the flames, he whispered to himself, well, that's it, God really is dead. Not crucified on a hill in Israel but burnt to death on a garden fire on the island of Portland.

The red tin he came across was taken downstairs and placed on the coffee table in the lounge. This contained the love tokens from his marriage. None of this would see the fire. Joy's wedding ring, her favourite necklace, their cards and love notes were all there. He came across a small envelope which held a dried flower, a lily of the valley. This was the only thing which wasn't related to their marriage. How did this survive?

Georgina, one of his congregation during his term in Dorchester, had given it to him. He had been married for about five years when Georgina had arrived from London. She had also been married but they had hit it off the moment they were introduced. Nothing had come of it, but the unconscious weight that something could have had been unbearable at times.

Georgina had been a member of the Bible Study Group and it had given them opportunity to meet and an excuse to stay afterwards. They had both known what was happening, but they had also known it couldn't happen. Neither had fallen out with their partners. Outwardly, their lives had been settled and complete. But Georgina, with her black hair and dark eyes, had held a power over him that he'd never before felt.

A kiss had broken the spell. They had been packing away the study books and their hands had met. They'd kissed and had stood there looking into each other's eyes. Nothing was said but both had understood. He'd never seen her again. The only evidence that that brief encounter had ever happened forty plus years ago, he was now holding in his hand.

The last thing he got to was the computer. He made the decision to delete every file he didn't use now. This meant almost all of them. Years of work were clicked into oblivion within a second. He was doing the same with his emails when, emptying the junk mail, he came across a message from the bishop. How it had passed him by and been dumped into the junk box, he had no idea. It was dated a few months after he had sent his dog collar back.

Dearest Matthew,

My motivation for writing to you is simple: I wanted to respond properly to your decision to retire from your profession, not as your bishop but as your friend.
 I have been a witness to your years of frustration and conflict with either your beliefs or with the church. I have seen you wrestling with your angel, struggling with doubt, with self-doubt and all done with a wonderful longing for the truth.
 I understand why you are ending these struggles now. I understand why you have decided to withdraw from the church you have been a member of since childhood. Naturally, I never wanted this and hoped that your discernments would lead to a reaffirmation rather than a rejection of your faith.
 Having said this, I want to make a confession to you. I envied your constant deliberations. I think you showed tremendous courage, relentless honesty and robust integrity. Sad to say but I think the church needs more people like you and fewer people like me.
 May I say, God Bless? Or, maybe, that is too much. So, misusing the words of the poet, I hope the eye of a little god will watch over you always.

"Could you put me through to Bishop Langton please?" He didn't expect anyone to be on the other end of the phone. "Tell him, it's Matthew Price."

"Who are you again?"

"Matthew Price, his friend and former locum priest for the diocese."

"Sorry to be so guarded but we have to check. I am sorry you haven't been contacted before; I am sad to tell you that the bishop passed away last month after a sudden illness."

"The virus?"

"Yes, I'm afraid it was. We were all so shocked. It was especially sad as he was due to retire in May."

Tia

Tia was up at four in the morning to finish her essay on Medication Options in Palliative Care. It wasn't her strongest subject. Getting to grips with it before the sun rose was quite a feat and yet, as Nara appeared in the kitchen, bleary-eyed and unable to speak, Tia pinged it off to her tutor.

Everything was about to change. Tia knew what all the world was becoming aware of. This may be the worst time or the best time to be training to become a nurse. This virus hadn't spread gradually across the world as with the old pandemics, this one had leapt about the globe, randomly appearing in places once deemed remote or distant. This wasn't a slow osmosis making its way from east to west, this was a firecracker, its embers setting off blazes as it hop-scotched its way from continent to continent.

Every country was unprepared and disbelieving, either blaming others or burying their heads and pretending it wasn't happening. Some thought that the right mental attitude would render them immune. Acting superior was an antidote to surrendering to infection, believing that this would skip by their doors like the angels in the Passover.

But the angels knocked on every door — and if it didn't open, they came through the windows anyway.

A lockdown was on the horizon. Already, Tia and all her year had been asked whether they wished to continue with their studies or to suspend them for a time in order to help out in the hospitals.

"You know what's going to happen today?" she said to Nara as energetically as she could.

"Yes," said Nara, wearily. "We're going to meet your boyfriend whose name is Harry Banks. You work with him and he will stay for tea."

"That's about it. Toast or cornflakes?"

She had been cautious with Harry — Louise had said "cautious to the point of ignoring him." In the past, she had blamed herself for picking dodgy men. She had certainly remained suspicious about her own judgement.

The open water swimming had continued, the group dynamics improving all the while, with two sub-groups emerging; the purists who were there for the swim only and the second group which enjoyed the social element afterwards as much as the activity itself.

Because of her domestic situation, Tia had been more inclined to belong to the first, although wanting to be a part of the second group, of which Harry was a member. Having a drink afterwards took a great deal of thought and organising and involved enlisting others who had already offered their unconditional support. When she had been able to pull it off though, it had meant spending some time with Harry. She'd tried to play down the mutual attraction, until eventually, her friends had picked it up and it couldn't be ignored.

Despite this, Tia had often been more relieved than saddened when Harry didn't make the swim or the drinks after. When he had come though, it had been obvious he'd sought her out. Her friends had kept taunting her, but Tia had held back, half terrified, half delighted.

The status quo had lasted until one afternoon when she'd been walking out of the hospital and was surprised to find Harry waiting for her. He'd looked tired and gaunt. His father had recently been unwell and she'd wondered if he had taken a turn for the worse.

"What in heaven's name is the matter, Harry?"

"It's you."

"Me?"

"Tia, I'm batty about you."

They'd started dating.

"About fucking time," Louise had said. "He would have been an old man if he had left it to you."

Every now and then Tia had to pinch herself. A few years ago she had been a typical single mum, in her early twenties, with a couple of kids and living in a shabby bedsit. Fast forward and she was now training to be a nurse, and courtesy of Matthew, the children were growing up nicely in the little house they could call home.

Compared to Harry's life though, she wondered if her lifestyle would be too humble for him. He owned his own place in Wimborne. He may feel that little old Weymouth was too working class—too candy floss and ice cream.

He arrived spot-on time. He later confessed that he had, in fact, arrived in town a few hours before, had found where she lived and then walked around counting the minutes until the appointed hour. He turned up with the largest bouquet he could have carried and chocolate for the children.

He had been there for about ten minutes when there was a knock on the door. Louise.

"I wonder if I could borrow some sugar?"

"Come in Lou and meet him," Tia said, opening the door for her. In she marched, straight into the kitchen, extending out her hand to be shaken.

"I'm Louise, Tia's best mate."

"Ah, Tia has said a lot about you."

"There's a lot to say. So, what are your intentions?"

"Louise Hornsby!"

"Just asking!"

"Honourable," Harry replied, laughing.

She stayed for a cup of tea, asking Harry direct and potentially awkward questions, which he took in his stride.

When she left, Tia started to prepare the dinner. She'd thought about takeaway, but she wanted to impress him with her culinary skills. She would make him a Mediterranean chicken dish with couscous. Whilst she was cooking, Harry played with the children. When they showed him their rooms, Tia crept upstairs and eavesdropped on their conversation. Through the crack in the door, she could see him on the floor, playing with the dolls and figures they were presenting to him.

During the meal, Tia was texted by Louise: *We're all fucked. The prime minister has finally and definitely announced the commencement of lockdown.*

"What are you going to do, Tia?" Harry asked.

"I've decided to go onto the wards."

"What about the risk to the children?"

"How can I," she said, suddenly irritated by his concern, "sit by and watch this happen and do nothing?"

"You must think of yourself first though and your own situation."

"That's for me to decide," she said, becoming unnecessarily defensive. "I have to get the children ready for bed now, so maybe it's a good time to leave."

"Sorry, I didn't mean anything," he pleaded. "I didn't mean to sour the evening."

"What's going on?" Nara chipped in.

"Nothing, Nara. Harry's got to go now, that's all."

Suddenly, they were saying goodbye on the doorstep. In his farewells to the children, it was clear he had made an impression. Kojo asked for a kiss which meant Nara had to have one too.

"Thank you for coming, Harry and thank you for the flowers. They're so beautiful." Tia said, rather formally.

Harry was looking nonplussed and a bit at a loss. "Tia, I truly apologise for messing things up. I'm not sure what happened but I hate myself for letting it happen."

She kissed him on the cheek and shut the door on him.

Half an hour later, the children settled into their beds, she went into the courtyard and rolled herself a cigarette.

"Fuck!" she exclaimed out loud. "Fuck and double fuck."

The overwhelming nauseous feeling was that she had majorly fucked this one up. What had she been playing at? His questions were perfectly rational ones. He was only showing an interest in her life. He was only thinking of the children, after all. Then it dawned on her. Lockdown meant they would not be able to see each other. Lockdown would kill off any hope of a relationship.

The doorbell rang. It would be Louise wanting a post-mortem. And, boy, did she need to talk it all through with her. She prepared herself for her jibes and criticisms. On opening the door, she discovered it was Harry. Of course, it was.

CHAPTER 9
January 2021

UK negotiations for a trade deal with the European Union conclude on 31st December 2020.

The Third UK National Lockdown to control the spread of Coronavirus begins on 6th January.

Trump loses the presidential election to Joe Biden by seven million votes but contests that it has been fixed.

Hundreds of rioters storm Capitol Hill, resulting in five deaths.

Scientists still insist the world has only ten years before we reach a climactic tipping point we will not be able to reverse.

Jon

Jon was woken by a loud thud on his bedroom window. He shuffled out of bed and drew back the curtain. It was still gloomy; the cold frosty world was waiting for the sun to rise. He couldn't make anything out until he noticed the fluttering black wings of a broken bird on the lawn below.

His usual response was to let nature take its course; this time he went downstairs. Opening the back door, it was obvious what had happened. A blackbird had flown into the window and was now stunned, one of its wings oddly angled and flapping jerkily.

When Victoria surfaced an hour later, she found her father nursing the distressed bird in his lap.

"Thank God, Vicky. I'm dying for a coffee but as you can see, my hands are full."

"Oh my god! What a beauty," she said, immediately relieving Jon of his duties. She deftly spread out the injured wing.

"No blood, which is a good sign. I can't feel any broken bones so hopefully it may have just bruised itself or pulled a tendon, or something of that sort."

"When did you learn so much about birds?"

"You wouldn't know this, Dad, but I have an A level in biology. We had to dissect one of his pigeon cousins."

"Shouldn't we call the RSPCA or something?"

"And what are they going to say? No," she declared, lifting the terrified bird to her face, "I think we can look after this fellow, can't we, you poor little thing? Get me an old sock."

"Excuse me?"

Jon did as he was told. She had him cut the end off and gently she pulled it over the small creature. It pecked her finger and she whispered, "Now don't be a silly boy. We're only trying to help."

"Well, I must say. I am impressed."

Watching her, it amazed Jon — and not for the first time — how you could literally live with someone for their entire life and yet not really know them. He was guilty of not taking either of his children seriously. Yes, he loved them both, but that was not enough, he could see that now. You had to be actively interested — no, actively fascinated — in their growth and development. That lesson had been too blatant and too trite for Jon to learn it. He could deliver a two-hour lecture on phenomenology without pausing, whilst the experience of deepening his understanding of the people around him was sadly lacking.

The first few weeks or so of the first lockdown had been bedlam. The two of them had been unable to synchronise their daily habits in any way which accommodated the other.

Lockdown meant there had been almost no opportunities to find the company of others. Peace would only come about when he had buried himself in his laptop and Victoria had been on Zoom or Facetime chatting with friends. She had been up until the early hours and had then spent the following morning dead in bed. Jon had been in bed by ten and up shortly after dawn. He had been on the verge of giving her an ultimatum.

The ultimatum had never been delivered. Victoria had started coughing one Sunday afternoon.

"Don't worry," she'd reassured Jon, "it's not Covid."

But the coughing worsened and by the morning, she'd had a high temperature as well.

"I think it is Covid."

"I think so too."

They'd checked the NHS site for the symptoms and then for advice.

"Ah, this is very helpful. It says don't go to A&E, don't go to or call your GP, just self-isolate. Call 111 if worried."

"I bet that neighbour of yours gave it to me. He looks like he's riddled with it. As soon as I'm in the garden he's perving over the fence, sneezing and spitting."

"Not sure it works like that, Victoria."

By the Friday, she'd lost her sense of taste and smell. Her temperature had remained above normal. He'd telephoned 111 and was given the same advice as the webpage.

"Am I going to die?" she'd asked him one night, after a particularly nasty coughing fit.

In any other circumstances, he may have laughed but it had been the young Victoria who had asked; the Victoria who was still eight years old. He'd felt a surge of emotion he hadn't experienced since he'd first seen her head emerging into this world.

"You're going to live forever."

In desperation, he'd contacted Tia and although she reiterated the standard advice, her caring tone did a great deal to pacify him.

"Just continue doing what you're doing. Keep her hydrated, that's important. She will be fine, Jon. She's young and her body will fight this battle for her."

Jon suddenly becoming the carer for his daughter, had helped them; it had slowed them both down and given them time to become content in each other's company. One night, when she had been feeling a little better, she'd come down to the lounge, determined to drink some wine. It had been the strangest experience: not to taste it or smell it and yet to feel the effects of it.

After days of little conversation, it had been Jon and not Victoria who'd begun opening up to her. He'd told her his story — naturally missing out some embarrassing details — but not avoiding how arrogant he had been and how low he had fallen.

Late April was exceptionally warm for the time of the year. The symptoms which had overwhelmed her for weeks had left, one by one, like disillusioned invaders who had decided to go home. They had begun spending more time in the garden. Reclining lounger chairs had arrived in huge cardboard boxes. They had discovered a little table in the shed so they could eat outside. Victoria had revitalised her passion for making exotic cocktails and Jon had dusted off the barbeque.

Gradually, almost imperceptibly, father and daughter had begun to tweak their own rituals in favour of a peaceful and easy routine. When lockdown had been eased, they had started walking and together they had explored the Purbecks and the New Forest. By June, they had been regularly swimming off the beach at Hengistbury Head.

Money had been a little on the tight side. Victoria had been furloughed as a barista in Southampton but had no intention of going back. Jon's savings had been chipped away at but he hadn't been worried, although he hadn't been sure why. He'd worked out that he could keep himself living like this in the rented house for three years, then he would be as poor as a church mouse.

In September, Grace had popped in. She too had been furloughed but was confident her work would be resumed sometime in the future. She had anticipated a huge catch up, a creative explosion, once the vaccine was developed.

"2021 will be a bumper year, you wait and see."

Grace and Victoria had hit it off at first sight. She'd become a regular visitor; she and Victoria frequenting pub gardens and going off for long walks. Jon had not been particularly surprised to find them walking hand in hand.

Victoria took the blackbird into the garden, following it around as it hopped on the lawn.

"I think we should keep it indoors for a couple of nights and then take the sock off to see if the wing has mended."

Hearing a loud knock on the door, Victoria picked the bird up in her hand and went to answer it. Jon was coming in from the garden when suddenly Sophie appeared in the kitchen shouting

"Daddy."

Lynda and Victoria followed her in.

"Well, this is totally unexpected."

"Guess what, Daddy?" said Sophie as she bounced around the room. "I'm coming to live with you."

"What the—"

"Thank you, Sophie," Lynda interrupted. "I was hoping to prepare you better than this, but events are taking over, I'm afraid. Sophie has been nagging me for weeks now and with this new lockdown, it makes sense. You're here doing nothing, whereas I'm busier than ever." Jon, for once in his life, was speechless. "What do you say?"

Victoria placed the socked bird onto the table. It hopped towards Jon, seeming to look at him, his head tilting slightly.

"I didn't quite expect this. A phone call, a discussion may have been appropriate."

"Come on, Daddy—can I come and live with you and Victoria and the bird?"

"After careful consideration," he said, marvelling at the four faces looking back at him, "I think it's an excellent idea."

Lexi

Rayn phoned Lexi to announce that 'lockdown numero tres' was on its way.

"It couldn't get worse. They take away our European citizenship on a whim and now another fucking lockdown. The good thing this time though, is that we're allowed to meet a member of another household. So, do you, Lexi Morgan, want to be in my bubble?"

"I thought bubbles didn't exist anymore?"

"Don't they? I just like the idea that I'm living in a bubble. Like a metaphor for life."

"Well, I hate to burst your bubble but I really think they don't exist anymore."

"Ha-ha."

She had barely survived the first lockdown. Lexi thought it was ironic that her illness, never successfully identified, treated or recognised, had imprisoned her in her room. Then from the world beyond Lyme Bay, a new virus, blindly aggressive and outrageously virulent, had done much the same.

At first, the good weather and Rayn with their little missions had kept her going, but these had seemed like brief moments which struggled to alleviate the endless hours of solitude.

She had taken it personally and seen it as a curse. She had been recklessly stroppy about the house, slamming doors, and picking unnecessary fights with her siblings. It culminated in a massive row with her parents about, of all things, putting tomatoes in her salad when she clearly loathed them and had done since year zero. She'd told them they were the parents from hell, that they had never done a thing to help her and that she'd wished she had decent parents like Rayn had. This had been doubly hurtful, as Rayn's parents were detestable snobs. When she had gone to leave, her mother had stood in the way.

"Do I have to remind you we are in lockdown?"

Lexi, pretending not to acknowledge this, had pushed past as her mother had let her guard down.

"I'm going for my exercise!"

"Only allowed an hour," her dad had shouted after her.

"Whateves!"

She'd walked to the woods, which hugged the cliffs all the way to Seaton. Happily, she'd found the footpath was deserted. She'd found her favourite beech tree and, sitting beneath it, she'd wept.

Way past the advisory hour, she had still been sitting there, feeling sorry for herself, when her phone had pinged. She'd admired Rick's persistence. Despite getting very little encouragement from her, he was apparently besotted and 'wanted' her. This text, probably due to the lack of feedback, was dialled down and merely asking where she was and what she was doing?

She had been getting up, when a thought had flashed through her head. She'd sat down again and texted him back: *Meet me now. In woods. In my favourite place.*

He'd appeared in less than half an hour. Finding themselves in each other's company, they'd both become shy and had struggled to string a sentence together. They had known why they were meeting, but neither had had a clue how to start. Eventually she'd taken his hand in hers and walked him up the high bank to a dip amongst the trees.

"This is my first time."

"Mine too."

"But I thought you were ... experienced."

"I pretended to be."

When she'd returned, her parents had been frantic. It had been more than three hours. Her mother had phoned the police who had advised them to contact them again if she hadn't returned by nightfall.

Seeing her parents so shaken had sobered her up. She'd realised she had to calm herself down and ironically, she'd begun to employ the same techniques she'd used to get through the days of her illness.

When the lockdown came to an abrupt and premature end, the world seemed to be in a race to make up for lost time.

Lexi went to see Ursula, who was trying to cope with the long-term effects of the virus. Rayn came along, supportive of her friend.

"It's so bloody silly," Ursula told Lexi, while her new partner, Greg, was out making tea, "I'm constantly tired but can never sleep. I have loads of great writing ideas, but as soon as I go to put them down on paper, my brain becomes treacle. Don't even ask me about my joints."

But, despite it all, she had clearly remained interested in Lexi and what she had been writing.

Lexi had brought a few samples at Ursula's request and just wanted to leave them with her, but Ursula insisted that she read one of them out. *Lyme Bay Blues* was the one she chose. When Lexi finished reading, she was surprised to see that Ursula was tearful.

"Lexi, seriously that was lovely. I loved the line ... the one about the harbour. The shore reaching its arms into the ocean, calming the waves in a hug. It's so brilliant, I have decided that I am not speaking to you again."

"What?"

"Until you submit that application for university. Just imagine three years of creative writing. I agree that Norwich is a long way, but so what? What you learn will be priceless and set you up for a lifetime of writing."

Greg had reservations, but Ursula was determined to take a walk along the beach with Lexi and the dogs.

"You," she told Greg, who had moved in with his mongrel, Hector, "are in charge of the hounds and we'll follow you up in the rear."

The tide was so far out; the beach had quadrupled in size, opening up beneath a sky of feathered clouds. Over the cliffs in the distance, somewhere near St Aldhelm's point, there was a lone column of rain, sweeping to the north. Seven large cruisers were imposingly positioned in a rough line from Osmington to Portland.

"It's the first time," Ursula said, seeing that Lexi was impressed, "we've ever had three Queens in Weymouth—Queen Victoria, Queen Elizabeth and Queen Mary."

The dogs couldn't believe how much the beach had grown. Hector wanted to say hello to everybody. Carlos rushed, as always, into the waves. Ahmed was non-stop, racing back and forth with the red ball he loved. Desmond kept to Ursula's side.

"I'm wondering how bloody long this long Covid is," Ursula grumbled. "The short version was bad enough but no, Ursula Bird had to have the long version."

"I suppose it's difficult to edit your book?"

"Oh, thank God and Jesus, that's all done. It's out there somewhere being polished and packaged. No, it's the new stuff I want to get to," she said, tapping her head.

They stopped for a moment to watch two horses being ridden by a couple of teenage girls. They were in the sea, almost to their bellies. Somehow, the sight of these two huge beasts in the water suggested something magnificent, something timeless and spectacular.

"But you know all about being frustrated, don't you, Lexi? The time of your illness must have been terribly confusing for you, such a hindrance. All that you missed — the anger you must have felt."

"Yes, I went through all those things. I think I hopped, skipped and jumped through the whole spectrum of emotions. I was chained to my bed. My body was going nowhere and yet, at the same time, my mind was everywhere. Sometimes I thought I was going crazy. Maybe I did. It was a form of madness at times. My room was full of ghosts and shadows. But there came a moment ... maybe not a moment, but some tipping point where I knew what I had to do. That was just to accept where I was and stop resisting or trying or fighting."

"Ah, Amor Fati. And did that work?"

"It helped when I realised that all those around me, my family and my mates, were experiencing all my emotions but second hand. They loved me, I knew that, but they felt powerless. That realisation helped to wake me up."

Ursula put an arm around her. "Don't upset yourself. I'm sorry to bring it all up for you."

"Don't be sorry. I'm not sad, Auntie, not at all. That was my education. I was saying farewell to being a child. It all had to happen the way it happened."

Their gaze fell on Greg trying his hardest to herd the dogs into a coherent group. The whole scene had become comical, as other people's dogs were circling and playing and sniffing one another. One cockapoo had run off with Ahmed's favourite toy.

"And that's how I became me," Lexi added.

One of the horses advanced towards them from the water. It wasn't until it was close that they saw that the rider was Rayn.

"How in hell's name did you get to ride the horse?"

"I knew one of the girls. I asked and she said yes."

"You really are a mad bitch, Rayn."

"Aren't we all?"

Dexter

The final straw was the New Year's party which wasn't a New Year's party. Despite this being the second year that Dee and Dexter hadn't organised their famous Hogmanay Festival, this year seemed much worse. At least the previous New Year had been spent drinking heavily and smoking dope in a stranger's house. It had won him the prize of complete oblivion he was so desperately seeking.

If it wasn't for the odd bloom of fireworks appearing randomly in the sky, you'd be forgiven for not knowing it was New Year's Eve. There were few people in the streets; those who did appear, wandered like ghosts who had been shut outside with nowhere to haunt.

Dexter was wandering the streets of a cold and empty town. The cruise ships in the harbour sounded their horns at midnight, but to Dexter, even that seemed tired and pointless. From the pier where he was watching, he could hear the hollow refrains from odd revellers, but he felt nothing and was content to feel nothing.

When he had contracted Coronavirus, the days laid up in the cupboard had felt like years. Dee had brought him round a meal mostly every day, or one of the boys had dropped it off. But there had been no physical contact. A knock on the door and there had been one of them waving at him, the meal on the doorstep. There would be a brief exchange checking how he'd been and if he'd needed anything. Then they'd gone and he'd returned to the gloomy interior, eating his food from a studio chair. Of course, the business had been closed and despite a government subsidy, he'd worked out that he would be going under in a few months.

On the fourth day of sickness, he'd awoken to find a note had been posted through his letterbox. Of all people, it was from Bernie Chivers. He had hardly seen him since the night Bernie had thrown him into the harbour. Somehow, Bernie had heard of Dexter's plight, and maybe out of guilt or kindness, he'd offered him the use of his father's old workshop at the bottom of his garden.

Since his father's death, Bernie had cleared it out of lathes and worktops and, with electricity and an attached loo, all that had been needed was a put-up bed. But, Chivers had added, he would have no contact with the family and they would have no responsibility for looking out for him.

So, his belongings again in a black bag, in one move Dexter had gone from cupboard to shed. The arrangement, both had agreed, was to last until his symptoms abated and no longer than four weeks. Nine months later he was still living there.

Finally, he'd tested negative in June. This had meant he could resume his weekly contact with the boys. Relations with Dee had been better than previously, but she'd never mentioned any plan for him to return home. When he'd brought up the subject, she'd told him straight that he'd known what must happen before she would even consider having him back.

"But I have had counselling."

"Four sessions—that's all you've had, and all before lockdown."

"But I have taken on board what was said. I have owned it all and know I have been a total fool."

"Explain to me then, Dexter, why Sherry Wallace saw you going into that house with a bottle of whisky in your hand?"

She'd been referring to the house belonging to Thirsty Kirsty.

"You know that I have nothing to do with her personally—I don't like her that much to be truthful."

"And yet you persist on going round there."

"It's not her I'm seeing. It's the gang of friends there."

"And that, Dexter, says everything."

Dexter had thought he was doing reasonably well. The last session with the old preacher had gone pear-shaped but some of what he'd said had stuck. Reluctantly, he'd allowed one notion to roll around his brain: that beliefs were merely a string of ideas that gave him a secure blanket to wrap himself in.

Dee had invited him for Christmas dinner. It had been bizarre being a stranger in his own house. On the one hand, he'd been familiar with every item of furniture, the scatter of ornaments and the rest of the household clutter, but on the other hand, being in his old kitchen, he felt slightly distant and insubstantial, like in a dream. After the meal, Dee hadn't ushered him out but had allowed him to relax with a beer in the lounge. When the boys had gone to their beds, she still hadn't asked him to leave. It had flashed through his head that this could have been the turning point he'd been waiting for. Would she ask him to stay?

"The boys miss you, Dexter. I miss you." Dee had been on her second bottle of wine.

"I miss you too."

"No, I miss *you*. Not what you have become. I miss the old Dexter. The one who I loved. The Dexter who was always laughing and messing about with the boys. I miss the old Dexter who loved to have people around, the Dexter who was a practical joker, the Dexter who would sit for hours drawing pictures while I watched TV. I miss that Dexter."

"I am still that Dexter," he said weakly.

"No," she said, taking a drag on her cigarette, "You are not that Dexter. The moment you began believing in all that shit was the moment that Dexter started to die. And worst of all, it was the moment our relationship started to die too."

"But we can have it all back, though," he said, stopping himself from adding 'if only you would let me back in'. "I've changed."

"Time for you to go."

Over the following week, he'd idled around, unable to focus on any one thing. One day he'd spent the whole time in bed, watching on his little box television set, everything from the breakfast news to a late-night film.

And now here he was, alone on the stone pier seeing in the New Year. With the virus still rampant and out of control, this one could be as rough as the old one. He sauntered to the end of the pier and looked into the noisy waves pounding below.

Except for the cruise ships, the sea was black and the sky full of heavy banked clouds. This was his town, his bay, his county. This was where he went to school, honed his skills as a tattooist, met Dee and had his two sons. What the fuck had happened?

He took the rucksack off his back and pulled out his laptop. With all his strength, he threw it as hard as he could. As it spun through the air, it opened. As he never turned it off, the light shone out like a lidded eye as it hit the water. For a second, he watched its brightness sink and then disappear completely into the darkness. He stood there for a while, in shock at his own impulsive action. When one of the cruisers pressed their horn for one last celebratory blast, Dexter jumped.

"Happy New Year!"

He became aware that a man on the pier opposite him was waving frantically at him.

"Happy New Year! Happy New Year!"

The man wasn't giving up. Eventually Dexter waved back just to shut him up. He turned back to face the twinkling lights of the town and began the long walk home.

Ursula

"The medical advice is not to commit yourself to anything too strenuous — and I think climbing white horse hill in your condition falls into that category."

By way of a response, Ursula stared at Greg until the man shrugged and left the room. He was beginning to learn that once Ursula made up her mind, even if the decision was unwise, nothing short of the amputation of her limbs would stop her. The last time she had climbed that hill was half a century before with her father.

During the long months when she had been incapacitated by this draining sickness, she had nurtured the idea to climb it again. The more she'd thought about it, the more it had come to represent a goal which, once achieved, would herald in a new chapter of her life.

All this time and hardly a word had been scribbled. Covid and the lockdowns had given her the best of all possible excuses not to write but it definitely had not given her the reasons. Lockdown, she had concluded, was an experiment in time. Time progressed no faster or slower than usual, but because it was metered only by the change of light and not by any events or interactions with others, the experience of it seemed akin to a wild gallop through the days. Something she had read or seen on television she'd put down as happening yesterday, only to find out that it had been a week ago, or more.

Anyway, she was on the up, and was enjoying more energy than normal. Today she was determined to climb the hill, even if it was the last thing she would do. Let Greg huff and puff about medical advice as much as he liked, she was adamant, and the dogs would love it.

Knowing that he was probably right didn't dissuade her but made her more resolute. After all, it was only seven weeks ago she'd had what she'd called a 'turn'. The medics had decided it was a respiratory event.

She had been wheezing all day, nothing unusual there. All she had done was let the dogs out into the yard but when Greg had returned from his jog, he'd found her lying on the kitchen floor, fighting for every breath. He'd told her he was phoning for an ambulance. If she could have responded she would have boo-hooed this and stared him out, but the choice was no longer hers.

As soon as she'd arrived at the hospital, she'd been put on oxygen. The immense relief of being able to breathe properly was exhilarating and if she could have spoken, she would have made a joke or two.

"Am I on my last legs?" she'd asked the first nurse who had come to see her the following morning. "Because if I am, I'd better start making my peace with Jesus or the Buddha or whoever turns up."

"The sheer fact you are making a joke tells me you may live another day."

The nurse had checked all the devices Ursula was attached to, then picked up her notes to record them.

"Hey, wait a minute …"

"Don't tell me I'd better start praying after all."

"Ursula Bird. You're Lexi Morgan's aunt, aren't you?"

"Great Aunt, would you believe? How do you know Lexi?"

"We were both speakers at a conference on children's mental health," Tia had explained. "Well, her friend was the main speaker. Now what was her name?"

"It's something to do with the weather."

"Rayn, that's it."

"Maybe Storm was her middle name? Rayn Storm."

"Ha, we got speaking afterwards and went for coffee. We're still in touch. Facebook friends. She's quite a talent, isn't she?"

"She's off to Uni next autumn, if the plague allows."

They'd kept her in for a week. Ursula had felt ready to leave on the third day, but they'd insisted on being cautious; her age and weight were contributory factors.

"Oh," she had said, "that's nothing to do with the virus. My age and weight have always been contributory factors."

Her lifelong friend, Jorie, had not been so lucky. She'd died the following week. On the Monday she'd started coughing with a slight temperature. By the Sunday, despite being on a ventilator, she was dead. Her husband, Michael, had been forced to watch the whole struggle through a window and then only at certain times. Not being able to hold her hand, or to kiss her, or rub her temples in a way only he knew how — these had been his sticking points.

"She was stolen from me. Kidnapped and slowly tortured. This was an unusual abduction—

not a vanishing, that would have been easy. I was a passive witness to it. I saw it all, the very life being drained from her. I was a spectator watching this person I loved disappear one bit at a time. Nothing could be so cruel."

Ursula had done what she could; comforting over the phone, contacting him every day. The funeral perpetuated the cruelty; only six had been allowed in the chapel. Social distancing rules applied; the ceremony had been brief, if not brisk. Ursula had made sure she'd spoken of her friend. Michael had been too upset to do or say anything.

She'd had to keep it short, so she did. In a couple of paragraphs, she'd recalled meeting her in the playground on the first day of secondary school, their trip to Paris, Jorie's wedding, the children, and finally their walks and conversations along Weymouth Beach.

She had asked Lexi to write a poem.

Loss is love's hard shadow
Without love there is no loss
Without loss there is no love

Loss is a show of love
Where the other cannot reply

Where the memory makes a try
To fill the place where they lived in your heart.

And your loss is a longing and a tribute of all you were
To me, to others, to the world
This loss is all I have
Your love fills it every time

It took them a good hour to prepare for the car drive to the bottom of White Horse Hill. Being herded into the back of the car, the dogs were uncontrollable with excitement. Desmond had to be lifted in but even his tail was indiscriminately whacking his companions in their faces with anticipation.

Ursula was about to lock the front door when the phone rang. Despite Greg's pleas to leave it, Ursula unlocked the door again and disappeared down the hallway. It was her agent.

"Good news! The book is coming out on September 1st. Plus they want to give you an advance of £10,000."

"What on earth for?"

"Yes, it is highly unusual for an unknown but they're thinking about keeping you for your second."

"Well, they may be waiting a long time for that."

"And that is not all. A film company is interested in getting *The Comfort of Blindness* onto the big screen."

"You're joking?"

"Not at all."

"The last time I said this word was in 1983, but I think it's called for. Fucking hell."

Ursula made it to the top of the hill. It took an hour longer than they had planned, but she made it.

"Except for the cruise ships in the harbour, this is pretty much as I remember it all those years ago. It's just beautiful, just beautiful. Not long after I was here with my dad, he died. He was a volunteer lifeboat man and he died in a rescue off the races, south of Portland. His body was never found. He really was lost at sea."

She hardly said a word on the way down.

"Is there something you want to say?"

"There is."

"I'm waiting."

"I know what I am going to write next."

"Better get back then," Greg said, smiling. "Before you forget it."

Matthew

Matthew was admitted in the small hours on the Wednesday after the new lockdown began. He was struggling with his breathing and unable to move. He'd had the sense to call Fiona, who'd called Tia, who'd called an ambulance.

By the time the ambulance crew had arrived, Fiona was waiting by the front door. He had wet himself. This had shocked him more than anything else and he had become tearful as they had lifted him into the back of the ambulance.

Since being sick with Covid, his health had never returned to what it was before. Ironically, the virus hadn't hit him too hard. His breathing had been the most worrying symptom but that was to be expected, considering his lifetime history of asthma.

After a month, his GP had said he was free from the virus and life could resume a degree of normality. He could actually allow Fiona into the house and some meals had been cooked in his kitchen rather than being deposited on his doorstep.

But the virus had left its mark. His asthma had been the worst since childhood and the fatigue which had hung round his neck like a weighted duvet, had been unbearable.

Despite his generally positive no-nonsense attitude, in the deepest part of him he knew something had changed and that the change was permanent and pernicious. His card had been marked. He'd jollied himself along with the notion that things could have been worse. He could have been in hospital, like so many poor souls, or he could have been dead. Why not? People were dropping like flies and the virus had been favouring the elderly with masochistic relish.

A couple of weeks before, he had received an unexpected visitor. The sudden heavy knock on the door had made him jump out of his skin. With a deep sigh, Matthew had folded his newspaper in half and made the long journey from the lounge to the front door. If he'd had his way, he would have left the door permanently open but Fiona had told him that would be pure foolishness. When he'd finally made it to the front door, he'd been taken aback to discover his wife standing there in a dog collar. At the same time, he had questioned whether the new medication he was on may be too strong, but this was no apparition.

"Hope you don't mind me popping round like this? I'm Zara Page, as from a month ago, your local vicar. You alright?"

Matthew had turned around and wobbled back to the lounge.

"Please come in."

Both seated, Matthew had regretted offering to make a pot of tea, but had been relieved when she'd declined.

"You sure you're alright, Mr Price?"

"It's nothing really. You remind me of my wife, that's all. When she was in her thirties. When I opened the door, I thought I was seeing a ghost. Maybe the holy ghost—with that dog collar. Who put you on to me?"

"Mrs Willis asked me to call. She said you were having health problems."

"Of course, I am. But I don't want to talk about them. I suppose she spilt the beans about me?"

"She told me a few things which I thought may help."

"Let me guess? I bet one of the things was how I used to be one of you."

"She did mention that, yes."

"What a surprise."

"I'm curious. If you don't mind, I would love to hear about your decision."

"Would you now?"

Matthew had told her his story. He'd found it liberating to talk about his loss of faith. Zara hadn't minded that he was taking his time. She had been the one who'd asked after all. He'd told her the story of his early conviction, his first doubts, Joy's accident and finally the death of Lucy.

Every now and then he called Zara, Joy. Every now and then he stopped short and marvelled at the resemblance.

"Wow! That is an incredible journey."

"Do you blame me for saying goodbye to it all?"

"Not at all. I have just read Henri Nouwen's *Spiritual Direction*. Have you heard of it?"

"Can't say I have."

"He says that God's presence is never separated from God's absence."

"Does he now?"

"He says the absence of God is sometimes so profoundly felt that it leads to a new sense of God's presence."

"Words."

"They're only words, unless they are true."

"More words."

She'd done a follow-up visit the next week. Matthew had been chair-bound and could hardly move without pain. Fiona had needed to be there to let Zara in.

"I'm taking a risk, Matthew, but I would like to pray with you."

"You're taking advantage of a man who can't even wipe his own bum."

But she'd seen that he was not objecting. She'd lit a candle and blessed it as the light of Christ. She'd taken hold of Matthew's hand.

Fiona contacted Tia to say that Matthew had been admitted into hospital as expected. In her breaks, Tia went to visit him, stroking his hand as she spoke to him.

During one visit, he rallied and was wide awake when she arrived.

"Ah, I thought you would come. I've been expecting you. You must forgive me. I'm not quite myself. I've been a little confused and distracted. But I've seen Joy."

"Joy?"

"Yes, she came to the house. I will tell you this. Come closer." He whispered into her ear, "she's as beautiful as she ever was."

Over the next few days, he drifted in and out of consciousness. Matthew would have loved to say his farewell to the world. There always was a sense of the dramatic about him. He would have made a grand speech, highlighting the ups and downs of a life rich in love and loss, but most of all celebrating the people who had been with him along the way.

No magnificent speech was forthcoming, only hours drifting between light and shade, where form became formless, shadows bent towards him, where soft words echoed in his head without meaning.

Tia was there at the moment he died. Before she alerted her colleagues, she kissed his forehead and thanked him. Then she heard what she could only describe as faint choral music. She stood up, staring at Matthew, expecting him to hover up and ascend to the heaven he had denied existed.

Then she realised it was not celestial or biblical in nature. It was not a summons from heaven but Radio 3 airing through Matthew's headphones. He would have loved that joke.

Tia

Finally, Tia was on holiday for a week. Holiday here didn't mean sun, sea and sand. In the nation's historic and unprecedented third lockdown, holiday meant time away from your workplace.

The first day of her holiday she spent all day in bed, floating in and out of sleep. The children were good as gold. At lunchtime, Nara made Kojo a peanut butter sandwich accompanied by an apple and a glass of squash. But towards two in the afternoon, they were becoming restless and when next Tia opened her eyes, she saw both children lingering at her bedroom door. Tia smiled and pulled back her quilt by way of an invite. They both jumped onto the bed, each trying to tell their mum a story about the morning's activities.

"Why are you still in bed, mum? Have you got Colin?"

Ever since the pandemic had begun nearly a year ago, Kojo, who was notorious for mixing up his words, had called Covid, Colin. The family now always referred to Colin. Absurd as it was, Colin seemed like coronavirus's lesser known but friendlier cousin.

"No, I haven't got Colin."

It was a miracle that she hadn't contracted it somewhere down the line. She had dealt with hundreds of patients by this time, some acutely unwell, some recovering, some dying.

The first dreadful month excluded, being tested every time she'd come on duty and having the correct protective clothing had obviously kept her safe. She'd already had the first of her vaccinations, with the second scheduled for April. Was the end in sight?

Like most of her colleagues, she was absolutely exhausted, emotionally as well as physically. She had worked most of Christmas, so this holiday was an oasis in a time of pandemonium and demand.

The autumn had been like working in a war zone. On her ward there should have been six nurses on duty at any one time. They'd had two: Tia, still technically only a student, and Beverley, an experienced nurse, twenty years her senior. Beverley had demanded that the ward manager do something to remedy this dangerous situation.

"It's a catastrophe waiting to happen."

Her response had been to get both Tia and Beverley in the office, leaving the ward attended by a couple of nursing assistants.

"Let me make it clear, no further staff are currently available. We have three off with Covid, one on annual leave—against my advice, may I add—and Kate is on long-term sick, as you know. Things will get better but at the moment it's you two and I forbid you two to go off sick."

Tia and Beverley had looked at each other in disbelief.

"I was joking," added the ward manager.

"It didn't sound like a joke."

"Well, it was. It's so important to keep up our spirits in these difficult times. Now don't let me stop you from your duties."

Tia had later found Beverley outside in the smoking area, but she hadn't been chatting and smoking as usual. She had been sitting in her uniform on the ground, sobbing.

"Is it wrong, Tia? I really want that fucking bitch in there to catch Covid and die a terrible death because there is no fucker to look after her." Her face was an estuary of smudged mascara.

"Beverley, you need to go home."

"You heard Adolf fucking Hitler, we can't go anywhere. Anyway, how can I leave you? It would be wrong of me, you're still a student."

"Go home. Just go. I'll tell her you collapsed, or a meteorite has hit your house, or your family has been kidnapped by mobsters. Just go home."

Without another word, walking like a victim of a horrific car accident, Beverley had staggered towards her car.

Of all the deaths she had witnessed, Matthew's was the one which had touched her most. Matthew had brought about a major turning point in her life. He had been a saviour to her and the kids. He had been a man who'd seen her as she really was, had understood her experience and had done something about it. She would always be grateful to him, always remember him.

When Fiona had contacted her to say he had been admitted to hospital, Tia had been there in her first break. Matthew had survived the initial virus but despite testing negative, it was obvious that the attack on his old body had irreparably damaged him.

Whenever she'd had a free minute, she was down to the other non-covid ward. She'd held his hand and spoken to him as if she had just popped into his little cottage on Portland.

On the few occasions he'd come round, he'd always given her a weak smile. He'd invariably told her that he'd been expecting her. Tia had reassured him that, of course, she would come. When he'd called her Lucy, she'd realised that he had been seeing someone else.

"I knew it would be you, Lucy, I just knew it."

The second day of her holiday, much to her children's excitement, she planned to meet Harry. Under the lockdown rules, one member of a family could meet a member of another family outdoors. With the children, it was a slight bending of this rule, which they were all happy to live with. Tia's relationship with Harry had been a turbulent affair. Not because they didn't get on well, there had been no problems in that department, but since they had met, they had experienced a year of lockdowns and restrictions. Harry had said it was like sharing her with someone else. The relationship had been off and on, without ever being turned fully off or completely on. But somehow, they had stumbled on regardless.

Though the day was sunny, there was a bitter wind from the east. The children were undeterred.

All buttoned up with scarves and gloves and woolly hats, they met Harry under their favourite tree in the Nothe gardens, overlooking Weymouth Bay and Portland Harbour. Three cruise ships were lined up, side on in a row. After the usual kisses and cuddles, Harry announced that he had hidden presents for them under the tree. Each present had their initials on it. This was the sort of thing Harry did and the children, naturally, loved it. Amongst the leaves or under the roots, the children found their gifts in about ten seconds. They rushed back to show their mum what they had.

"Aren't you going to get yours too, Mum?"

"Oh, one for me too?" she asked, raising her eyebrows at Harry.

It didn't take Tia long to find her gift, but when she did, to the children's surprise, she suddenly ran off up the hill. She joined the top path and ran down to the fort. There she stopped and opened up the little red box which housed her gift.

A ring.

She found them sitting on one of the benches overlooking the sea.

"Where did you go, mum?"

"I needed to clear my head."

"And is it clear?" asked Harry.

"Perfectly."

THE END

www.ingramcontent.com/pod-product-compliance
Lightning Source LLC
Chambersburg PA
CBHW070458120526
44590CB00013B/678